Friends and Lovers

Julian Sleigh

# Friends and Lovers

*Working through relationships*

Floris Books

First published in 1988 by Floris Books
Second printing 2002

British Library CIP data available

ISBN 0-86315-267-8

Printed in Europe

# Contents

# Foreword

My aim has been to share with you thoughts and experiences which I hope will help to enrich your relationships and deepen your understanding of yourself in these relationships. They are not meant to be fixed propositions but a stimulus for personal exploration.

Here and there I have drawn upon aspects of the spiritual science of Rudolf Steiner, aware of the need for a fuller treatment. This is available in the literature of Anthroposophy.

I have also referred at some points to The Christian Community. This is a widespread movement for the renewal of religion in our time, which celebrates the seven sacraments in a new form.

My thanks go out to many colleagues and friends who helped to expand my ideas and encouraged me to share them. And I want to pay a warm tribute to my closest and most valuable relationships, to Renate my wife and our children, all now grown up; they have helped me to keep up with changing times.

J.C.S.
Cape Town.

# 1. Setting out

There are warm places in every person's soul.

These places can be filled with feeling for others, and those others can be aware of this feeling. Something passes between persons who carry in themselves a warm feeling for each other: feeling itself flows through those souls and unites them. And openness towards this power of feeling enables the warm places in each person to be alive and active.

Friendship can only exist in such warm places.

Friendship is a phenomenon, deserving our reverence and awe. It is a gift that each one of us can nurture; it does not just happen. It is precious.

We shall dare to explore this phenomenon. We will touch on areas of soul experience that are tender and not easily put into words. We can search for guidelines that help a person to grow in love, expanding these warm spaces and rejoicing in the power of feeling. Thereby we will strive to reach an understanding of togetherness, and find a way to achieve commitment in friendship that is in line with the freedom that rightly belongs to a modern person.

We live in a time of reassessing all forms of relationship, the institution of marriage, the way of effective parenting, and the place of sexual freedom and constraint in daily life. We are challenged to find solutions to this maze that are clear, radiant and self-sustaining. There is an earnest urge to become masters of the art of harmonious interacting.

Those who watch the apocalyptic signs, and study the evolving freedom of Man as an individual, note the prophecies of a coming 'war of all against all.' Battles between tribes, tension between economic blocks, racialism and conflicts between nations become less central in the concerns of peacemakers. Though many such conflicts still dominate the political scene, the essential problem becomes increasingly domestic.

Many human beings are proving unable to live purposefully and at peace with a freely chosen spouse. Children are suffering from the lack of parental skill, and tend to reject the feebleness of persons in authority. The general level of trust among friends, acquaintances and fellow-workers has markedly declined in the western world. And more and more people are suffering from a gnawing soul-loneliness. Attempts at forming communities show how difficult it is for people really to share and to co-operate without sacrificing their freedom and their yearning to be individuals.

Something brilliantly simple can teach us about relating, understanding and supporting one another: you have it built into you, and so have I. Our two hands. See how they are with each other, how they relate naturally yet perfectly: the one hand may lead, the other follows. They accept each other all the time, totally; they never get in each other's way. There is grace and harmony in their togetherness; each has its own strength and weakness, but they compensate and complement each other. They give us an ever-present yet ever-changing image of companionship, togetherness and friendship. And it all happens so silently that we take their skill at relating for granted. There is a deep wisdom and a heart-warming dynamic in this mutuality that is inscribed in each of us.

# 2. Being a complete person

What do we wish for, and need, for our self-esteem? How do we attain a feeling of fulfilment? How can we take hold of our everyday self and through it find access to our Higher Self? Such questions have to be answered before we can build lasting relationships with others. A right relating to ourselves needs to come first.

It is not easy to attain fulfilment. We have to work hard on ourselves to become well-directed, focused persons, able to cope with events as they occur and to transform setbacks into valuable experiences that broaden the scope for future achievement. Anyone who strives for fulfilment will realize that this requires a process of self-development. This process covers five essentials.

A basic need is a sense of purpose. This may sound obvious, but how many of us can make a clear statement about the purpose of our life? Platitudes come easily to mind, but they are only vaguely related to our aspirations: they are no substitute for belief in the purpose of our own individual existence and trust in our ability to accomplish it. These can only develop out of our own discerning sense of destiny.

Can we read the signs in our biography that reveal our mission? The place where we were born, the family, the clime; the formative events that have unfolded in our biography so far, the rhythms and repetitions that have patterned our life-story, the events that have helped or hindered our progress; our gifts and weaknesses, our doubt and confidence, the conflicting goals of our ambition: all these spell out the message that points the way to our own life-task.

Nothing special will be achieved if we set goals for ourselves but fail to marshal the forces and sharpen the skills that can attain them. This is a matter of will power. The will is a mysterious force in the human soul. It can all too readily be enthralled by our habits and predilections, indeed also by addictions, and so be largely unfree; it needs our devoted effort to wrest it free from these unconscious constrictions, so as to render it responsive to the guiding thoughts and images that stem from a higher level of soul. This requires constant motivation and application: only through self-discipline can we achieve the mastery of conscious aspirations over the unconscious drives within us.

The way to personal fulfilment will remain closed to us until we achieve a clear sense of purpose and the self-discipline to guide our soul-energies.

The aspiring person must then make sure that his resolves are not subject to swings of mood. It is all to the good if life-happenings fill him with joy and enthusiasm, but not if they make him madly euphoric; and there is no harm in a certain pensive inwardness, as long as it does not sap his initiative and sink him into depression.

Contentment and fulfilment require a balance in the feelings so that we do not lose control. Equanimity safeguards the person from being carried away. Anger, anxiety, shame, are not only upsetting and hampering to the soul; they undermine the health of the body and cause it stress. An equable mood avoids pent-up breathing and strain on the heart, and so enables the instrument to serve the guidance of the higher self. But all this calls for constant attentiveness.

A fourth need of a well-functioning person is a positive attitude towards all that we are and all that comes to us.

There is good in everything: rightly worked upon, even something intrinsically evil can release a hidden fund of good. The same magic touch can lead ugliness towards beauty, untruthfulness towards truth. The eternal qualities of goodness, truth and beauty can be discovered in everything we meet, however negative it may appear: a positive insight will release hidden value, which can redeem the ugliness, the wrongness and the depravity. Such striving for positivity creates a channel for the flow of feeling. We experience life as good and true and beautiful, and this has its effect on all our relating: others are drawn to us, and we meet them with empathy.

The fifth fundamental quality that prepares the way to fulfilment in a person is openness. For friendship and the building of relationship, openness is vital; but it needs to be worked at all the time, and occasionally by an extra-determined effort. In particular this affects our way of accepting another person in our life. (This aspect will be explored later.)

Yet openness means more than reaching out to another person: it means readiness to learn from everything, even from unlikely sources. If we resist new experiences, reject new ideas, and repel everything that would add new content to our thinking, we lose contact with our higher self: and without this contact, we shrink and harden and eventually dry out. If we are prepared to change our patterns, we make way for the influence of our higher self. This leads to the enriching and fructifying of our own ordinary self: we realize who we really are, and we can express this in our daily life.

These five ways provide the muscles necessary for fulfilment. They are based on five of the six basic exercises that set a seeking person on the path of inner development. The sixth is the harmonious interaction of the other five.

To recall these five ways:

— a clear vision about oneself
— action guided by self-discipline
— an equable mood
— a positive attitude
— openness to meet and learn what is new.

# 3. How am I doing?

Before relating to another person we have to relate to ourselves. This is the foundation of all relationships with others. Indeed the strength or weakness of all other relating depends on the state of our relating to our self.

Solitude, as compared with loneliness, is a beautiful state, especially when it is freely chosen in circumstances of real silence, peace and natural beauty. Each person is inherently a loner, and this healthy alone-ness asks for ongoing renewal and cultivation. Though embedded in a family, surrounded by love and supported in life, a person needs to have times of 'coming to self': times of aloneness even if it feels like loneliness. There is a primal need to be alone for periods of contemplating and prayer, for thinking, digesting of experiences, for writing, and for renewing one's resolves. Even the act of reading for leisure requires the withdrawal from interaction with others: we need to be alone, to be left alone, to have our aloneness respected. Only thus can we replenish the soul-strength that enables us to give to the world around us.

It must become possible for us to hear the silence, and this is difficult wherever mechanical noises pervade the environment: all our energy-savers are noisy! We have become accustomed to electrical devices that relieve us of life's daily sweat and toil but we forget the price we pay for them. They are a constant drain on our nervous energy, and they have an uncanny ability to barge in whenever we seek for quietness. Compare the sound of a sickle or shears in gardening to the noise of a motor mower or an electric strimmer.

Yet even if aloneness and quietness are both possible, to be wholly silent is often not. For there is also the turmoil of our own emotions. The worries and fears, the longings and disappointments, the dents and bruises suffered at the hands of others, the rejection and sense of failure: each has its distinctive tone that adds up to a cacophony in the soul. We may be unmindful of the tumult while we go about our daily work, and there will be plenty of distractions at odd times in between: but when these are absent the cacophony seizes its opportunity. We need to bring all this to peace before our solitude can heal and renew the energy of our being.

It is not easy to bring peace and inner stillness to the soul. One way is through becoming clear about the issues or memories or worries that trouble us: when we think about them, we wrest them from the clutches of our emotions. Clear thinking can be stimulated by conversation with a good listener, or by writing a description of what is bothering the feelings: either way we become creative. Or we may turn to some form of art that directly engages our true originality. In such a way we make it possible for the matter to be offered up to the divine element that surrounds us all. Our life is enriched when we are able to contact this other dimension, and let it help us to work through and pacify our experiences. None of us is totally alone, for the spiritual factor in our lives accompanies us in daily existence, and we may call on it. The channel is thought: it can guide us when we turn to it in silent openness.

This activity can bring us to the creative spring of our own being, the place in our soul where we link with the universal wisdom and the creative energy of the spiritual world. But for this channel to open we have to clear out all prejudices and preconceived ideas: all fixed attitudes that restrict our openness. These are obstacles to the free working of our thinking. It is scary to let go of standpoints that bolster our conception of the world, yet to have the courage to do so enables us to move from a stagnant pool to a rippling stream. Without such courage we can only find security in holding on to a 'position': but imagine the freshness that can enter us when we are open to new thoughts and inspirations from our own inmost fount of wisdom!

This means discovering the poet within us. Becoming persons who see everything that comes to meet them as containing a deeper mystery, a message, a healing and a guiding image. Such persons keep their fantasy alive and bring healing to their surroundings: they can derive a feeling for the good from the purity of their thinking activity.

When we can experience the stirring of moral fantasy within our personal inner life, we will know the value of times of solitude. Once there is an ear for the inner voice that speaks softly yet clearly within the soul, a voice that is free of emotional stress or guilt or fear or shame, then we come into touch with our 'better part,' the Higher Self, the eternal part of each of us. This helps us to allow the sounding through, the *per-sonare,* of wisdom, healing and right motivation into our earthly conscious existence.

Then each of us becomes a fuller human being:

— free of dependence upon other people, or upon institutionalized systems or fixed standpoints;
— free of co-dependency resulting from the unconscious adoption of certain patterns which tend to dominate our behaviour like an addiction;
— free of the conditioning influence of our upbringing:

race, nationality, family style, political propaganda,
restrictive religion, habits born out of uncertainty,
and the like;
— free of shame: a painful experience that comes from
deep within us when something we want to cover up
is stirred and exposed, and makes us want to disown
ourselves;
— free from a backlog of unresolved stresses and therefore able to respond appropriately to current happenings;
— free to live.

A poor self-image is a sign that the person is not yet aware
of the true Self beyond his everyday self. He is not yet in
touch with infinite beauty and goodness and truth. He
finds the way forward when he is able to recognize who he
is, and rejoice.

There are many thinkers who have identified this potential in the human being to rise above everyday existence
and infuse it with qualities that lie dormant in the soul: a
potential waiting to be woken that will raise a person to
ever greater heights of human worth.

This was recognized in the Renaissance by such writers as
Pico della Mirandola, a member of the group of philosophers
around Lorenzo the Magnificent. Pico wrote of the human
being as able to fall beneath the behaviour of the beast, but
also to aspire to the sublime power of an angel.[1]

Earlier this century, Rudolf Steiner wrote that every
person is potentially able to attain the power of seeing
spiritual realities.[2]

And Abraham Maslow, who died in 1970, developed
the concept of self-actualizing to signify the enhancing of
a person's own performance, which would then open up
the full use of his potential.[3]

Such expansion can only come about through times of solitude. And only when we learn to welcome our insights, even though they challenge existing thought patterns. And when we are humble enough to listen to what comes towards us from the world around.

# 4. Openness

How can we find the way to get on well with each other?
What must we do to acquire the skills and attitudes that
foster harmony and friendship? What can bring about a
relationship that is purposeful and pleasing? If we could
find an answer to these questions we would help mankind
to reach the age of brotherhood. And make our own life
more meaningful.

A first step would be to examine how it is when persons
interact. We do not often stop to think about how we
relate; we become conscious of the effects, and then
maybe wonder why the encounter has been pleasant or
unpleasant. To be fully in control, aware of every step we
take and of the dynamics that ensue, could have the effect
of distracting us from the reality of our meeting with one
another. But we can look back while the event is still fresh
in memory. Let us try to analyse what happens.

We meet someone. There is contact through the eyes,
maybe through hands and a form of greeting, often
instinctive, which straightaway sets the tone for our interaction. Our faculty of feeling is the first to be engaged: it
is quite mysterious. If this is destined to be a significant
meeting, the feeling in us will flow out to the other person,
and feeling will flow back to us. What this interaction conveys will depend on the circumstances and purpose of our
encounter and on how we are with each other. A true meeting goes through several steps of recognition and
acknowledgment, and the space we give to this will affect

the success of our interaction. We see each other, feeling flows; we recognize each other, we acknowledge each other; we exchange verbal or non-verbal greetings, we converse.

Our conversation may not remain on the same level throughout the meeting, but we are likely to set out with one of four modes. Our conversing can be on a thinking level. Then it can remain objective, with facts or ideas as our subject matter. We meet 'out there' in the realm of thought. The way we share the thoughts can lead to a greater closeness or to clinical distance. At worst the exchange can become blocked by disagreement and come to an end, with our agreeing to differ or just differing and giving up. Alternatively, thanks to an effort to understand, the ideas and thoughts can develop, become clearer and fructify each other. Two people coming from their individual past and present state of being can tune in to each other's thinking and meet in a pleasant way if they can hear each other and not be fettered to their own reaction. So often we are caught up with thoughts that arise in ourselves, and we react to what the other says: 'I don't think you are hearing me' is a common complaint. Listening in to the thought-processes of another is a faculty that requires real effort and a selflessness that gives clear space to the thoughts spoken out by the other person.

Suppose the other person makes a statement and we disagree vehemently. Our settled viewpoint is threatened, and we move into the offensive. What rubbish! And he's got a nerve to say such a thing! It takes courage to climb down and move alongside, asking him to share his view with us more fully. If we accept the challenge we give ourselves the chance to widen our horizon and thereby to grow. We may end up humbler, but also wiser and more truly confident.

The very word 'under-stand' has in it the gesture of 'supporting from below.' If we can understand like this, the other person will find himself confirmed as a person and will not feel he has to identify with his proposition and rise to its defence. The proposition is now between you as your joint concern. You have shown interest: now you can look at the idea together, not as antagonists. His pride-involvement subsides, and maybe he is now prepared to re-evaluate what he had stated. Your further conversation together will be enlightening for you and for him.

How come? Because you have been *open*. You have shown that you are prepared to learn. You are not threatened or disempowered nor put onto the defensive by the exchange, and nor is he. You have listened; he too may be open and want to consider your doubts about the proposition. Your relating will grow in depth and warmth: there will be no space for antipathy, dissidence and conflict to rear their ugly heads.

So far we have remained in the thinking mode, and the threat to this was safeguarded by your openness. Any emotional reaction would have disturbed the process of striving for truth, and given rise to another kind of interaction: for when the emotions are stirred, objectivity is lost; it retreats into its own safe ivory tower to await a more congenial climate.

But what can we do if the encounter is emotional from the start? The person who addresses us vents his feelings (as distinct from 'feeling' — see Chapter 12) against us, or possibly against someone else, in the hope of gaining our sympathy. If the emotion is based on anger or anxiety, either will be disempowering to that person: one aspect of his gesture may be an appeal for help to restore reason in his turbulent breast. Anger is often felt to rage in the stomach; the physical body takes the strain.

Here our openness will lead us to recognizing the emotion *per se,* but also to seeing the person who is temporarily in its grip: he is a different entity from the actual emotion. We can observe quietly 'you are not your emotion.' This means being open to the person, despite his emotional state, encouraging him to speak out all that is upsetting him. But while he is in the emotional state there is no value in arguing about what he says, or in responding by saying 'No! That is not true.' For him, at this point, *true* is what he feels, not what you say it is: his feelings are his reality.

As he begins to describe his plight and you ask him to go into detail, or to explain what the matter is, he will be called upon by his own reason to think about what he is saying and feeling, and gradually his reasonableness will reassert its sovereignty. You will have confirmed his worth as a person.

Your aim is to help him to be a free, authentic, self-directing, balanced and open person. However dimly, he will sense this and will look to you as his example. You fail him if you yourself react emotionally to his emotion. And if you criticized his behaviour he would feel himself bombarded but not met.

Then there is the mode of feeling, as compared with emotion. If someone expresses to you what she feels, you can destroy that openness with a clever remark that comes from your cold objective thinking. A child may show you a golden autumn leaf in the fall, and wish to share her delight in its beauty, and you reply 'It is only a dead leaf; put it down.' You will put her down and deaden something in her feeling soul for ever: and you will lose the chance of an experience that the child could have given you.

We can understand the hurt we cause to others in such ways if we remember how it is when we ourselves are at the receiving end. Often at a concert, when the music stops after its sublime finale, you can give yourself up to its after-image: until suddenly your companion crashes in with a critical remark about the soloist, or even quite naively asks 'Did you enjoy it?' Bang goes your reverie; you are not allowed to remain in feeling mode! Or else you want to let a friend understand you better, so you share with her a feeling of sadness about the way things are going, and she responds by saying 'You know, you should not feel the way you do; it is not really like you say it is.' That is quite a gentle, almost a 'feeling' response, but nevertheless it does not meet you where you are. You will feel denied, and will stop being open because you have not been met with openness.

I was once deeply troubled by something that had happened to one of my children, and a well-intentioned and wise friend said to me 'But don't you see? It is her destiny that this should have occurred.' That morsel of wisdom did nothing for my pain. I learnt through this never to douse feeling with a thought. Never try to rationalize a pain away. It is a human privilege to be vulnerable, for then the truly human in a person can be reached. However, this needs utmost care and understanding. In another word, openness to feeling (see Chapter 12).

It is interesting to notice that while a person is in feeling mode she cannot easily use words, unless she feels really in tune with her listener: only if the person she communicates with is a listener. And not only a listener to words, but one who observes and discerns the feeling that is coming from her, the resonance, the deeply-ordained gesture! Often silence is the way to say the most; the gesture that conveys: 'You don't have to say more, nor do I; we are in communion.' This is more than being in communication.

However, the closest way of relating can be through

deeds. We can converse and communicate through our thought-filled words; we can share how we feel with another through poetic speaking or through our gestures. But when we work together at something, and achieve results through our co-operation, that brings about the deepest relating. By working together we forge bonds. It may take adjustment, discussion, emotional exchanges; but once we have done what we had set out to do, or have surmounted difficulties together, an unspoken connection to each other comes about. When friends or partners feel a distancing happening between them, giving rise to estrangement and mistrust, there is nothing so effective as getting into will-mode together, helping each other to achieve something meaningful through a joint effort. The sharing of exertion and being able to experience the good feeling of achievement are important. This restores openness to each other.

Openness is not passive: no-one can be forced to be open. The person has to open himself; any coercion is abuse. Yet openness is generally unconscious. To make it conscious requires an awakening to the mysterious dynamics of relating.

We need to grow in consciousness if we are to become masters over the way we interact, for only then can we ensure that we do not hurt one another or generate conflict in our everyday existence. As individuals we are no longer held in check by our families or folk, by our personal or group *daemon,* by the furies who used to control human consciousness from outside, or by a determining collective subconscious. Many of us have also emancipated ourselves from the strictness of religion that required confession of sins and the constant awareness of our trespassing into the space belonging to others. All this is because we are emerging to free individualness, which places upon each of us the responsibility to act consciously in our dealings with each other.

Yet we often rush headlong into relationships. It is as if we feel the urge to unite with others, submerge into a larger whole, cast away the freedom that mankind has so laboriously developed: alone we seem to find it too difficult to keep control over our own words, gestures and deeds. We surely need contact, communication and also communion with others, but without consciousness and self-control this relating may result in confusion, conflict and coercion. It is striking how the small prefix 'co' can signify our coming together so positively and at the same time heralds so many difficulties. But such is the precariousness of relating.

Our study of openness is only a first step in finding a way to develop the skills needed for relating. Each of us can try hard to be open in a conscious way, but the right dynamic can be established only when the 'others' also try. Yet my conscious openness to you will help you to trust yourself to be open to me. And we can enter into an agreement about the way we will relate; we can accept it if either one of us points out where we are lapsing into the old unconscious mode of interacting (and reacting). We need to overcome the natural shyness about exchanging views on such matters; it is necessary to cope with any embarrassment or self-consciousness. It is easier for me to ask myself 'how am I doing?' than for you and me to ask each other 'how are we doing?' ! But it is helpful if we can manage this. Then the openness is mutual and our relating will be enriched.

| | |
|---|---|
| Thinking to thinking | This is congruent.[4] |
| Feeling to feeling | This is harmonious. |
| Willing to willing | This is positive. |

If too much will pervades my thoughts they could destroy yours through my being forceful or critical of yours. This way I can squash your self-esteem and throw you into confusion, until you either succumb to my ideas or distance yourself from me. In this way my thinking can be thoughtless! I may emerge imagining that I am the cleverer of us two, but I will have caused hurt. Why? Because I have not been open to your being, your sensitivity, nor your thoughts. We have not built a relationship.

My thoughts can equally destroy your feeling by responding critically and cleverly to what you are expressing sensitively from a deeper place of your soul. We have surely all experienced being put down like this.

My thoughts can work on to your willing, causing you to be constrained, unfree to act, lamed, de-motivated. I can paralyse you with my cold intellect.

I can also undermine all your soul-openness with an emotional response, my anger, anxiety, impatience, rudeness, lack of interest, disdain, jealousy. All these close me off from responding to you. They destroy openness.

My will working on your thinking will brainwash you.

My will working on your feeling will deny your very selfhood.

My will working on your willing, either suppresses you, enslaves you or causes a violent clash.

So if we are to tune in and be together in harmony, we need to be on the same level of soul, and be open to each other. Our thinking together will bring about communication. Our openness in the sphere of our feeling will promote our wellbeing. And our working together will generate communion. If these arise out of balanced mutual openness, we will relate in freedom, without pressure. Our communication will engender discussion, agreement,

understanding. Our feeling well with each other will overcome loneliness and strengthen our regard for each other.
Our mutual communion will bond us into community. The
result: a positive feeling of love. Then our relating will be
generous; we will each rejoice at the wellness and achievement of each other. Our hearts will expand and also our
courage to be.

# 5. The dynamic of affection

At the marriage feast of Cana the wine was all used up. Mary told Jesus about this, and he replied in a way that is difficult to understand. He said: 'What to you and to me, O Woman?'

This has been variously translated as: 'Woman, what have I to do with thee?' (RSV); 'Your concern, Mother, is not mine' (NEB); 'That is no concern of mine' (REB); 'You must not tell me what to do, Woman' *(Good News for Modern Man)*.

The Greek is very spare, even cryptic. But the two datives indicate that something is weaving between mother and son. And this has to do with the Woman in her, opening the way for him to take action, involving a miracle for which he feels unprepared. Mary is wholly satisfied with his reply and feels able to instruct the servants to carry out his commands. Indeed the water is changed into wine.

'Something is weaving between you and me;' in this case it has to do with the relationship between Mother and Son, between Woman and Man. There is the hint that Jesus is dependent on his mother, but in the action that follows we see that through the event he does become independent. The love between them is infinitely strong. This same love will be shown by the Mater Dolorosa at the Crucifixion. Jesus speaks to her and to John the beloved disciple from the Cross: 'Woman' (again he addresses her as Woman, not as Mother) 'behold your Son' — meaning John. This same love makes possible a new step in mankind's development: <u>humanity transcends blood bonds</u> and can begin to form new, free, purposeful associations of a deeply spiritual but also of a human kind.

<u>Nevertheless it is first of all blood bonds that give rise to attachment and affection</u>.

To belong to the same family, to grow up together facing the joys and sorrows of life, thereby developing a loyalty towards each other, is a basic source of attachment. The ideal of a full or even extended family, possibly with three generations, a large house and a set of 'familiar' rituals to ensure harmony and purposefulness, is seldom found today in any modern or semi-modern way of life. The large family was the training-ground for overcoming selfishness and provided a secure base for all the members, so that respect and mutual understanding could be learnt and practised. But in step with the unfolding of personal individualness and personal growth, each person has nowadays to take responsibility for his or her own life. Consequently the large family has been replaced by much smaller units: often single parents with one or two children, or couples without. Dwellings have shrunk to a small number of small rooms in blocks of flats. And the cohesion of families has declined. However, blood ties are natural and will always feature as a generator of human attachment and affection.

But, further: <u>what makes me like you</u>? I may feel good in your presence, and also feel reassured by you even when you are not near. There is something radiating between us which I like and cherish. It is not something I can explain; we have no blood relationship. But maybe we have climbed a mountain together, or gone through the valley of difficulty and have helped each other across. Yes, there is something about you which I like, and I feel it is mutual. I think it has to do with the way that we 'see' each other; we have mutual 'regard.' You fit my image of the friend I wish to have; you enable me to feel valuable. There is something working in our relationship.

This sympathy could not be entirely fortuitous: merely a lucky coincidence, a gift of harmony. We may understand this in a deeper, more mysterious way if we are open to the idea of karma. Then we begin to recognize what really happens when people meet, and to see what lies behind companionship. It all makes sense if we can grasp that we are drawn together by the working of destiny.

Because of a situation in our previous lives on earth we now meet each other in this one. After our death we had each reviewed the life we had lived through: we saw what we had done, yet at the same time we could feel what the other had experienced. We realized how much had gone wrong or been left incomplete: and this kindled in us the longing for a new opportunity to put things right. Often we had caused hurt or pain to each other: now we could feel the suffering we had inflicted, and we are keen to make amends.

Or this same life-review might have recalled a purposeful meeting that had not fulfilled itself. A different kind of incompleteness, and this too left us with the wish to meet again; so in our next life this comes about and we both know that we are destined to work together. Or maybe the review brings back to us a brief experience of mutual love, in circumstances that caused it to be denied; but now we are attracted together again, and this time we can celebrate our love, and maybe even fall in love. Many such intentions came together and formed the karma that we brought with us into our present life. They were the guiding force behind the meetings that have been woven into our life-pattern. Only we do not know it: all consciousness of this was blotted out when we were born.

These ideas may seem strange, even alien, to those who have not considered the possibility of repeated earthly lives. The cornerstone of Eastern spiritual conviction is the law of karma: our misdeeds affect us in the life or lives that follow. Any hurt inflicted, any debt left unpaid, any harm we have done, calls for a deed of compensation in a subsequent life. This means that the people we meet and the events that happen in our life are not a matter of chance but have been ordained by the law of karma: we are given the chance to redeem and clear the negatives in our previous biography. If we fail to do so, a karmic 'debt' remains to be cleared in a future life. Hence karma is considered to be an iron law.

This century a Western spiritual science has come through Anthroposophy, made known by Rudolf Steiner. This sees Christ as the Lord of Karma, bringing about a compassionate working of destiny: the iron law is replaced by the encouragement of unselfish love, with which we can assist each other through the hard crises in life. This idea of karma does not take away our free will. Karma can bring us together, enabling us to meet and interact. But the way we do so depends on our own decision here and now, on our own behaviour: for this we have to take full responsibility as individuals. Karma can never be blamed for our actions and conduct: it can be felt as an impelling desire for a deep and intimate relationship, but how we respond is our choice.

Another strong force that draws people together is of course the dynamic of sex. This does not have to mean the promptings of sexual desire. The phenomenon of the division of the sexes is deeper and wider than the drive to unite with another person so as to experience a strong bodily or emotional sensation. What has to do with reverence and understanding for another person will have a different feel if that person is of the opposite sex. This applies regardless of age differences. Our natural sympathy is aroused, and also our power of caring. So the sexual element can be a source of attachment because the other sex is always somewhat of an enigma wrapped in a mystery. It is intriguing and calls up responses at many levels. We will be examining sexuality in greater detail in Chapters 18 and 19.

There are few persons who are not vulnerable in regard to their self-confidence and self-esteem. Those who seem really secure in themselves are often covering up a softness, even a hurting, that they feel but do not want to reveal. We are all weak, and we may try to cover up our inadequacy. But our weakness is human. The very essence of being human is that whilst mankind is the crown of all creation, endowed with a spark of the divine, it is far from complete in its development. A person's potential for growth of soul and spiritual enlightenment is unlimited.

Humanity is destined to bring about a reunion of heaven and earth, with help from spiritual entities, the angels and the higher hierarchies working in the service of Christ. Christ's teaching, His Words, taken up by human souls working on earth, will culminate in a 'passing away' of the separateness of heaven and earth. His guidance has not only been collected and written in the Gospels: it resounds in the promptings of our inner self when we allow them to be heard in our soul's life. These promptings, this guidance, will be given to all who develop an inward quietness to receive ideas and impulses that can lead us in the working out of our individual destinies.

Our daily life, shared with others to varying degrees of intimacy and openness, provides a constant opportunity to glean wisdom and enlightenment. Life is a gradual initiation, and at crisis-points the learning is intensified. We are all on a path of growth, stimulated by what comes to us as experience; we strive to achieve through our own effort and intention. If we were already perfect there could be no growth; but as we are not, and can grow, we are vulnerable and insecure. Someone who believes he knows it all will ward off contradictory experiences and block further growth: he is a sorry sight.

Thus weakness can become our greatest strength. It helps to keep pride from submerging us; it enables us to realize how little we can achieve alone, on our own, and how much we depend upon each other for the fulfilment of our aspirations. This need for each other opens us to feel grateful towards those who help us and accompany us, also towards those who see our weaknesses and make us aware of our failures. Such gratitude can feed a long-standing attachment; it can also open up a deeper connection with someone who had been only a casual acquaintance.

'You meet me but you do not invade me.' We long to be met, even more than to meet. This being met confirms our worth and stills the shame, anger and anxiety that lives in our soul. By being met, regarded, accepted, even admired and loved, we dare to accept ourselves and to open ourselves more confidently to our own inspirations, our own personal inflow of ideas. This is a healing experience when these ideas are new, fresh from the source of ideas: archetypes and impulses that bring energy and enthusiasm with them. In this state of reassurance we can be open to changes in our familiar life-patterns.

This shows that we have great power over each other. We can confirm or deny each other's validity: we can encourage and liberate energies and talents by our regard, or deflate by our poor opinion. Naturally some people are more easily affected by the attitude of others, and a person who is over-sensitive will be less effective in life. Yet even the great and the strong are influenced by the degree of respect and warmth of regard which they receive: not necessarily only from their equals and those above them, but from anyone to whom they are in any way open.

It is as if we need constant reassurance that counteracts another force, a prompting that comes from within us. For indeed in most people there lurks an imp or a wicked step-mother who tries to undermine their self-confidence. This voice, sometimes snarling or sarcastic or superior, taunts its victim with remarks like, 'you are not doing very well, are you?' or, 'how on earth do you think anyone is going to listen to you or take you seriously?' It can be worse than this: it can be totally laming. This built-in retarding factor makes itself felt at certain critical phases like the age of twenty-eight or the mid-life crisis around thirty-five to forty-two: it is a challenge that can sap our strength. But if we can sift out the truth of its message, without being deterred by it, it can stimulate our growth.

Someone who has a real insight into human nature can help a friend by staring this imp down, causing it to relax its grip on the jugular of his self-confidence. Such help can be offered instinctively as a by-product of affection and love. But as mankind goes more and more towards individualness and consequent isolation, the gaps between people need to be bridged by conscious feeling. We will then recognize many others around us to whom we can convey the same message: 'You are valuable; you are full of potential and I do recognize something of the true *you* in you. I challenge the imp that wants to undermine your feeling of worth.'

Not always can we accept to be met. We may feel this to be an intrusion, paralysing our freedom and cramping our space. Respect for boundaries is of great importance. We can feel invaded due to inadequacy and vulnerability, or more positively because we do not want to give up our integrity. Meeting has to be based on mutual agreement. And the one who takes the lead in meeting the other must be prepared to be met himself.

Granted these considerations, meeting one another can be a source of deep enrichment. Because we do not only meet what we see in one another, we meet in an exchange of feeling. And there is also something intuitive, even partly psychic, in the meeting of eyes, and the vibrations that intermingle. We convey to each other a reminder of our shared humanity, our inheritance of a wise evolution and our potential for infinite growth. This happens in a true meeting: we sense the true being, the Self of the other. This experience can be a flash of recognition, hardly entering our consciousness; or it can be cultivated, so that every real meeting with another person can be a sacred event.

If we could achieve this way of meeting and being met, we would become aware of our own spiritual nature, and of the guiding spirits, the guardian angels, who actively engage in such moments. The memory of the other person remains imprinted in us, and a seed is planted in our souls, the seed of friendship. True meeting gives rise to loyalty, regard and understanding, which all contribute to the mystery of friendship.

# 6. Friendship

And so, what is friendship? How is the transition achieved from being an acquaintance to becoming a friend? What does it mean to befriend another person and to receive his or her friendship in return?

A friend is a person who is prepared to suffer in support of you: to suffer for you and sometimes even to suffer because of you. Your friend will give you space within his soul, and carry you in this space. If this is mutual a bonding comes about, enabling you to touch his feeling, to affect him, and he you. This can give pleasure through the melting of aloneness, or can be painful, when the plight of your friend becomes your own burden because you are open towards him. So friendship gives rise to both joy and sorrow, to helping one another but also to increasing the burdens that you take upon yourself.

Yet these burdens are accepted freely: friendship is not bondage. Once the relating becomes unfree, feeling can no longer flow: as soon as a sense of obligation enters into the relationship, often accompanied by a sense of guilt or moral pressure, the true quality of friendship is punctured and begins to drain away. If the one appeals to the other by saying 'Surely you will do this for me after all I have done for you,' the friendship is in danger. Certainly a person may feel he wants to help a friend who is in crisis, but this has to be a free decision on his part: otherwise an element of manipulation can come into the relationship.

Awareness of each other's needs belongs to a healthy friendship: and practical assistance, freely offered and accepted, can only strengthen the bonding. But help rendered out of a sense of obligation entails a threat to the friendship. Everything that feeds a friendship originates from the heart and can only be sustained in freedom; any pressure is destructive.

This makes friendship precarious, for it can all too easily be drawn into a state of demand and obligation. Then, imperceptibly, bonding changes into bondage, and togetherness becomes constricting. From time to time friends need to ask each other: 'Am I trespassing on your tolerance?' The state of a friendship needs constant watching.

Friendship cannot be routinized: and this will happen if it is no longer fed by an inflow of feeling. It requires safeguarding, cultivation and openness to the new: to be kept alive and vibrant it needs care and maintenance. At times it will become sick, wounded or exhausted, and so will call out for healing; it is sad indeed if it becomes terminally ill and there is no further hope.

The healing of friendship is therefore a matter of re-establishing the element of freedom and the flow of feeling. To prevent it from suffocating a strangled friendship will require:

—   the renewal of mutual understanding. We have to ask 'Where are we now? What is it that is causing our estrangement?'
—   the dissolving of blame and resentment that may have built up on account of probably minor misunderstandings. Are we willing to discuss our situation openly with each other?
—   the re-establishment of contact. Have we simply lost contact through involvement in other activities,

allowing a vacuum to come about? Friendship is vulnerable to vacuums.

— the re-enlivening of communication. Any breakdown in relationship has a communication-problem nestling within it. Friendship cannot exist without communication. A blockage in communication will block the flow of friendship.

In everyday language we 'make friends' with a fellow-worker, with the new next-door neighbour, with someone we are introduced to. But real friendship comes to us unexpectedly. We meet, as though accidentally: yet there is an immediate feeling of kinship, which readily ripens into friendship. Or long-standing acquaintances share in some dramatic situation which makes unusual demands, and they find themselves meeting in a new way on a deeper level. When such a meeting opens the door to friendship, it is easy to say it was a lucky chance how this or that event brought us together. But the hand of friendship that reaches out between us takes the place of a word that need not be spoken: 'This had to happen; we'd been looking for each other even though we didn't know it.'

There is a kind of recognition in that look into each other's eyes, as though to say: 'Maybe this is our first encounter in this life, but we've been together on the earth before.' And we may get a glimpse of the future: 'There will come a moment when distance or death once more brings separation, and yet we will remain connected and will meet again in time.'

Such recognitions give strength to true friendship: but friendship has to undergo severe trials to prove its

endurance. There may be months or years when circumstances deny all possibility of contact. And even if it is
fairly possible to meet regularly, hindrances are inevitable:
distractions interrupt far-reaching conversations; emergen-
cies trespass on planned opportunities to be together. True
friendship survives such petty hazards, and transcends
geographical separation which reduces frequent contact to
occasional letters. It needs to prove that it can stand up to
this without falling into a vacuum. There is a shared
tacit understanding that this is part of the testing that
friendship has to submit to, and that it can only lead to
eventual growth. There is some truth in the saying that
absence makes the heart grow fonder.

Friendship, once kindled, acknowledged and deepened,
can flourish even with minimal sustenance on far-apart occasions: one meeting links on to the next, even if years have
rolled by in between. The level of communication is only
heightened by the specialness of the long-awaited meeting.
All that has happened in between becomes unimportant:
what counts is, 'Now we're here together again.'

Friends in contact with each other can share each other's
on-going situations. For them there may be a different kind
of testing. There may be times when one friend needs to confront another about some task that he obviously should
address but is neglecting. It will hurt his pride; sudden
awareness of one's own defect is painful. Such pain is like a
searing, searching light that pierces the murky darkness of
one's semi-conscious soul. But it is potentially healing: it
may be the only way to uncover what is detrimental. The
very fact that something is pushed down, covered up, seemingly forgotten, gives it an undermining force: it remains as
unfinished business which hampers the soul life. No person
can afford such clutter in his psyche. But who is to bring it
to awareness? It has to be someone who knows the person

and cares about him. Even so he takes a risk: he can anticipate that even his friend may be tempted to blame the
messenger.

Unfortunately most of us tend to blame the messenger
for the bad news he brings. We may retort with an indig-
nant 'How dare you tell me this! I know it already deep
down, but I did not want to admit it to myself consciously,
nor to bring you into it. Have we become friends so that
you can pry into my hidden soul? Oh, I know there is a
mess, but it is mine and I don't want intruders. You make
me uncomfortable.'

How different if the person can breathe deeply, compose
himself and respond by thanking his friend for his concern
and for the effort he made to bring the matter into the day-
light. Now that he can admit the truth, his friend can offer the
balm of empathy and compassion: and this will give him the
strength to face the newly-awakened realization and make a
plan to transform the negativity into something positive. And
he will be able to acknowledge the help he has received.
'Now I know that you are a true friend: you confronted me
when I needed it, and so helped to heal a weakness and
redeem a wrong state in myself.'

If there is no acceptance of the truth, the friendship may
founder abruptly: 'I never want to see you again!' If the truth
is accepted, the friendship can blossom silently.

# 7. The wonder of the soul

Relating is not only an artistic endeavour; it is a discipline. It calls for the creation of a suitable space between you and the other person, a space that you both can freely enter, enjoy and share. Yet it also requires you to conduct yourself in a way that leaves the other person free: or, better, enhances his feeling of freedom. You cannot constrain other persons to relate to you; you can only offer them the space, invite them to use it, and hope that there will grow an understanding and a warmth between you.

No-one except a hermit can live in isolation, yet each person needs his own space: a home ground that is safe and under his own control. It may be small, and its boundaries hardly discernible, but the person must be able to feel that it is uniquely his. Often we invade the space of others: we are well-meaning, seeking contact and wanting to help; but we invade. We fail to knock at the door and await the call to come in; we ignore the fact that the space does not belong to us or to the world but to that person. If we treat it as if it were common ground or even a part of our own space, we are in danger of arrogating to ourselves the privilege of entering.

We are not speaking here only of a physical space — a room, a house, a property. A private possession of this kind is a symbol of the inner space in the soul of each person. We are speaking of that private area which is mine alone, that part of me that can pronounce the word 'I.' It is this part of myself which gives me integrity, congruence, authenticity. I have to take hold of thoughts, grasp them and let them become mine. An inspiration, or a thought offered by another person or gleaned from a book, has first to be received, acknowledged, taken hold of and learnt. This is a process similar to digestion. Then it can be assimilated into my own being: I can generate a thought of my own out of my own soul-working, which is shaped and formed by the content I received. I build a new thought of my own, after the image and likeness of that which came to me. Then I can say I have thought this idea out for myself. Just the opposite of brainwashing. So thinking is a process of creating one's own thought content out of all that is understood through our senses, stirs in our emotions or comes down as inspiration. This process of thinking and gaining our own standpoint or system of ideas is very satisfying. But it does imply that we grow in respect for the differing standpoints of those around us.

It provides one way of developing an inner space that is truly our own. The space of our own personal thinking can be like a laboratory, a library and a peaceful garden all in one: a place where research and ordering of knowledge can happen, and where one can work in a living, growing spiritual landscape.

This means that whenever we want another person to do something we ought to address him and present the need or request in such a way that he can receive it, understand it and share his response with us, so that the final result would be a joint decision. Then instead of complying with our directive he acts in freedom, able then to draw upon the deep store of energy and devotion that lives in his soul.

The humanizing force in our soul is feeling. My own inner space is the place where I find my Self, a place where I can experience my worth and my meaning. It is a place which contains my own work-in-progress: my unfinished work, my personal ideals, but also my feeling.

Feeling is a stream of active soul-substance that is different from thinking and willing. We have to distinguish feeling from the feelings. The feelings are part of our emotional life; they are personal, arising in our soul as reactions to whatever moves us. Feeling is a stream of spiritual force that enters our soul when we are at peace with ourselves and with the world around.

Feeling dissolves all aggression. There is sensitivity for those with whom we associate: we can honour their space and welcome them into our space. This is considerateness, a step towards overcoming selfishness.

The person who acts out of feeling is no autocratic ruler, cannot be a boss; but, like Jesus in the Sermon on the Mount, he or she speaks with authority, with what in classical Greek is called *exousia.* A power that is mild, well-intentioned, allowing, respectful, dignified, in a word, gentle. (The English word 'gentleman' captures this meaning.)

In no way is a feeling-person feeble. Or lacking in the best side of concentration. When a person concentrates on a task, and allows feeling to work into the thoughts and impulses, a special artistic element comes into the activity. The task may be demanding, but it never becomes hectic or exhausting to the nerves. It draws out the enthusiasm of those who are involved, leaving them free to generate their own purposeful energy.

Feeling enables a person to revere. Reverence opens the way to interest and insight: it gives empowerment to the one who is revered, enabling him to reveal the hidden secret within; it illuminates a flower or a work of art, so that its secret also becomes apparent.

There we have the vital point. Feeling, when it flows,

empowers. Empowerment is the essential ingredient for social relating, and it has to do with this force of feeling. I cannot think my thoughts into you, and I had better not put my will into you: both would make you subordinate, a puppet. But I can call into myself the power of feeling, and relate to you in this mode. Then if my attitudes, intentions and desire for compliance are held back, and I honour you and share my concern with you, the power of feeling will convey itself to you, and your soul's reaction will be positive. This conveying of feeling is an art, a skill of our heart, one that needs careful and sustained nurturing. Our openness to feeling requires schooling of the heart.

The physical heart, far from being a kind of pump, is an organ of perceiving. It senses the intake of oxygen from outside and the experiences of the blood within; it registers the rhythm that relates the two together. Deep within the physical heart is the soul heart: this too is sensitive; it relates our inner soul experiences to what we draw in from outside of our organism. This heart, we could call it our poetic heart, is the sensitive organ for all our relationships.

And indeed, relating signifies the on-going adjustment of soul-forces, so as to maintain harmony. Poetic means creative; our soul-heart has the task to monitor all the dynamics that play into our relating with each other. The physical heart keeps going non-stop, but it depends on the coronary arteries to bring it energy and sustenance. The heart that belongs to our soul-life likewise depends on continual regeneration. Its task is daunting and continually challenging: without such sustenance it becomes weakened, saddened, burdened, lamed, and even ill. It may suffer silently, but its need is great.

How can help come? Through that kind of activity that

brings feeling into the soul. This heavenly substance is the only one fine enough to filter through into the soul-heart. This substance is spiritual, and it is called *love,* in Greek *agapé,* which signifies the highest form of love: spiritual, selfless, unrelated to personal enjoyment or satisfaction but also unrelated to anything that can be commanded. It is exemplified by the question Parsifal asks of the suffering Anfortas: 'What troubles you?' It is caring, sacrificing, totally giving.

This means that this love, like feeling, is given to us; it is not something we can generate at will by ourselves. The love that overtakes us, fills us and radiates through us, in a way that spreads warmth and joy, is a gift from the heavens: it enables us to transcend our selfishness. As this is perhaps the noblest aspiration mankind can have, love is indeed the greatest gift the divine world can bestow upon the earthly one.

Yet it is the human being who can provide the conditions for love to work. One of these is the freedom of will enjoyed by the human person.

Love cannot be forced or commanded. Many translations of verse 34 of Chapter 13 of the Gospel of John are unfortunate. For instance RSV: 'A new commandment I give unto you: that you love one another as I have loved you.' The word *entol* has to do with achieving an end, making perfect; *telos* means fulfilment, completion. So Jesus gave an aim towards perfection: I give you a new aim that will bring fulfilment and perfection. Love one another.' He uses the word *agapé.* This is a gift carried by the flow of feeling. Not always is feeling impregnated with *agapé:* the world would be a much happier place if it were so. But our innermost heart bears within it a latent capacity for selfless love. This has to be engendered by the striving for openness on the part of the human soul: only this openness can enable it to become the bearer of love. It is an offering, a calling upon the higher world to grant this gift. For it to be poured out by the spirit there needs to be a vessel, a channel to receive it and convey it further. Every human being can be a channel for divine love: but the channel needs to be clean and unblocked. To achieve this entails suffering or self-denial. Hence this highest form of love implies sacrifice, the 'laying down' of one's life for one's friends.

The openness to *agapé* and the receiving of the joy and sorrow it brings with it lift a person from a state of self-indulgence and self-absorption to a level of being that is noble, generous and inwardly resolved to serve the good. Such is the grace of *agapé*.

Love can also mean a cheerful giving and taking on the level of our everyday humanity: the enjoyment of friends, the engaging in satisfying activity that brings about interaction, sharing and mutual support. Indeed it is friendship: the form of love called in Greek *philia*. The heart is warm, loyalty and interest are nurtured; the ups and downs of daily life can be met with buoyant openness.

The word *eros* has given rise to 'erotic': but eros is not a desire driven by our sexuality for the sake of sexual fulfilment. It has to do with passionate delight and ecstatic admiration. It contains the element of excitement and the striving for possession; the eros condition has more to do with wanting to be loved than with loving. In *eros* we have the expression of emotion, with its warmth and power. It is not selfless: the self-sacrifice it impels is no more deliberate than when the moth flies into the flame of the candle. The power of feeling as we have outlined it here has much to do with *agapé*, a little to do with *philia*, and hardly anything to do with *eros*.

To become a civilized person means refining our openness

to the flow of feeling, enabling it to reach through us to our companions and to all objects of our care and affection. The more this feeling can be the bearer of *agapé*, the more a person brings warmth, harmony and empowerment to those around him. This can work as a healing force, a blessing.

# 8. Helps and hindrances

To develop togetherness and companionship with someone it is certainly a great help to be able to see each other regularly, and on such occasions to be able really to meet. Contact and communication fills the spaces that can otherwise become vacuums, which draw in many of the darker, less positive emotions; without such contact we can find the picture of each other fading, or taking on garish distortions. Doubts can undermine our trust in each other, and there can even be resentment: 'Why doesn't he write?' 'I think she has forgotten me or turned away from me!' A relationship needs to be seen as a living entity that grows or declines: it is not static, fixed, solid. Like any living thing, it has its biography; it is constantly changing as it grows older, and its state of health will vary according to the circumstances that impinge upon it. So it is not always true that absence makes the heart grow fonder: a long separation, and the erstwhile friends may really move apart; the friend of before becomes irrelevant now.

That is unless a deeper connection has come about: a spiritual bonding which is not dependent on human meeting in the flesh, in the body. Even so, the dynamics of biographical growth work against a maintaining of companionship, for with every two people there are at least three sets of dynamics: the changes taking place in each person, and the growth, change or decline of their friendship, as an entity in itself. It is true, as we have seen earlier, that when two friends meet again after a long separation it can seem that it was only yesterday that they parted: but that is generally not the case. No-one remains the same in the dramatic stream of time. The phenomenon of ageing, the impact of each day's experiences, the expansion and contraction of the sense of who one is, are continually having their effect. All this brings about changes in the formation of one's soul. If friends do not keep up with each other's changes, the former perception each has of the other can be restricting: 'You see me as I used to be, not as I am now!'

Then there are other obvious hindrances that can undermine or destroy a relationship. A difference in age, previously unimportant, may eventually present a barrier: a man going through mid-life crisis, or a woman in menopause, can seem a stranger to a former friend. Or the belief systems of friends may suddenly diverge. Two friends who were mildly unreligious may go through contrasting conversions, the one becoming a born-again Christian and the other a devotee of New Age ideas: the latter would thereby become totally unacceptable to the former. Or divergent political views could cause rifts when sensitive issues gain sudden importance. A further hindrance to togetherness can be when the one person comes under stress through problems in the sphere of his work, or meets a humiliating turn in his fortunes, or suffers a rift in his marriage: such a changed situation may have nothing to do with the friend, but there is a spin-off effect and communication breaks down. Or still more decisively, when one companion marries, the other must stand back and give space for the new relationship to establish itself.

Such happenings have to be reckoned with: they are part of our daily experience. Maintaining a relationship can frequently be hindered by adverse circumstances. What is commonly needed for a relationship to prosper is availability: if the friend is no longer available, the togetherness will be made difficult and the friendship may wane. Sometimes this is to be welcomed, for persons may have to move on in order to grow, and not stand in each other's way. As there can be nothing fixed about a relationship, it is constantly in flux, waxing and waning like the moon.

And there is yet another aspect to consider. We have touched on the phenomenon of karma (see p.32). Once we accept that karma has an influence on our life we begin to recognize that any meeting, person to person, has a reason and does not happen by chance. The reason can be a karmic debt, requiring us to meet so that what was left unfinished in a previous life or went wrong, causing grief or hurt, can now be put right. So we meet, and through the 'energy' of karma we are attracted to each other. This provides the chance to interact purposefully. Thereby the debt can be paid or the hurt is healed.

When this has been completed, and the slate is clear, the energy that brought about this meeting may subside: suddenly, or gradually, it ceases to work. If, in the course of our relating, we have not developed a selfless interest in each other, but unconsciously relied on the karmic energy, our friendship could now founder: 'We don't seem to have so much to do with each other any more!' Such a distancing can bring about the atrophy of our relationship, without a discernible reason. This is why a knowledge of the working of karma is helpful. Our initial attraction and its eventual decline need to be accompanied by a recognition of each other out of freedom. This recognition enables us to safeguard and nurture the relationship. Then, when we become aware that we have no more old debt to each other, we can rejoice, for we will know that our friendship is now released from the obligation of karma. From now on it can be based on a love that is free.

When this stage is reached, something else can gradually

become apparent: this friendship is not now based on the personalities of the friends, but upon something deeper and more constant. Once a friendship has reached the level of the spiritual essence of a person, it becomes a state of being and is not jeopardized by circumstances in daily life and passing fancies. It becomes a commitment which grows through the challenge of hindrance and adversity, as much as it flourishes under the warm sun of a satisfying connection.

We can now turn to this kind of higher friendship.

# 9. Soul-mating

Why is it that most of us do not allow ourselves to be known through and through by anyone else, even by friends and spouses? There appears to be an inner core that is not to be entered, like the Holy of Holies. Maybe because no-one really knows what is concealed in this inner sanctum, so we safeguard the space: either in the belief that it would be desecrated by anyone who enters into it, or in the fear that it is, in fact, empty, void. This latter is a worry that is not spoken about, but it exists, and vibrates through the being of a great number of people.

In spite of this barricading of that central core, there is a deep secret longing in many souls for someone to come, in peace and friendship, and to enter into this hallowed space so as to share it with its owner. This is the place of greatest aloneness; it is the inmost self. In Matthew Arnold's poem called 'The Buried Life' he describes in sadness how rarely a person can truly be himself and be true to himself thereby.

> Only — but this is rare —
> When a beloved hand is laid in ours,
> When, jaded with the rush and glare
> Of the interminable hours,
> Our eyes can in another's eyes read clear,
> When our world-deafen'd ear
> Is by the tones of a loved voice caress'd,
> A bolt is shot back somewhere in our breast

And a lost pulse of feeling stirs again;
The eye sinks inward, and the heart lies plain,
And what we mean, we say, and what we would,
    we know.
A man becomes aware of his life's flow
And hears its winding murmur, and he sees
The meadows where it glides, the sun, the
    breeze ...

In such an instant:

An unwonted calm pervades his breast.

Moments of calm like these are rare: but when they happen, then we become aware of the flow of feeling from one person to another. There is no human experience to match the wonder of such moments of communion. Saints and mystics can experience communion with the divine; but, for all of us, deep relating person to person, meeting and being met, could happen more often than it does. Surely it need not be so rare for two people who are friends to know consciously what it means to be close in this way? Out of deepest respect and selflessness they can confirm each other's deepest worth. Love-making in the sexual sphere is an image of this coming close to the core of each other, but is no substitute for it: this is the lie that most modern people labour under.

No, the true meeting of I to I in safety, in unwavering loyalty, in deep understanding and support, in full regard for the eternal in each other, in total reliability, this should be possible to men and women in our time who are free individuals, self-actualizing, rounded personalities, congruent, yet aware of their shadows and weaknesses. They should be able to soar in their truly spiritual selves to the heights of nobility and love, and so touch the truth in each other, undisturbed by sexual and emotional self-indulgence, and then descend from the heights bonded by a covenant that will never break: for they have dared to meet the good in each other, and the beautiful.

But, as Matthew Arnold says, this is rare. For such a sublime meeting will be tested and threatened, and many demons will rise up and try to undermine the courage or adulterate the soul state. They will lace it either with a cloying sensation of delight or a beastly desire for power or will want to shatter the experience into a thousand broken pieces, leaving the friends distraught, defiled and devoid of integrity.

So this way towards meeting the soul of each other  needs inner preparation. Any spiritual achievement requires an equal if not greater development of moral clarity. It needs self-knowledge, a developing acquaintance with both our higher Self, the eternal part of ourselves, and our lower self, the fallen part. Our higher Self has the task  of redeeming the lower self, transforming the energy of our selfishness into the force of selfless love.

——— o O o ———

We need each other if this world is to be filled with love. The selflessness that this implies can help to transform the fallen state of Man into one that bears spirituality.

When demons influence men — or, worse, possess them — they can become violent, or full of guile. These demons feed on our weaknesses and suck away our energy for doing the good. For demons are tortured beings, puzzling and pathetic. They actually want to be released from their torment; they need our compassion and love, and they drink in any healing power we give them. When

demons are freed from their fetters, they can become helpful to man, or just dissolve. Their negative working is
prevalent in our modern civilization, and individualized
persons are especially vulnerable to being invaded by
them. It follows that any effort we can make to overcome
our selfishness, and to love one another with true interest
and dedication, helps to redeem the demons and so clears
the atmosphere of this kind of pollution. We all benefit,
and especially our children.

Moreover, whilst it is easy for humans to love their dogs
and cats, their possessions, and all that they enjoy from
nature, it is difficult for them to love one another. The scal-
ing of the heights of intimacy and inwardness described
above can never be attained before a person admits his or her
own weakness. Relationship is precarious and insecure until
the weaknesses are shared. No-one is entitled to demand of
another that he reveal his weakness; but if two people wish
to associate, they will gradually become aware of each
other's weaknesses, and there will come a moment when
they can speak openly about them. Then, in that instant,
friendship will either arise or will be blocked, possibly for
always: for our humanity is tested by the way each of us
responds when another reveals his weakness. Do we assert
our obvious superiority, with scathing criticism, sarcasm or
crushing comment? Or do we seek to understand, to sense
the vulnerability of our companion, and to regard him all
the more positively because of his honesty and congruence?

Another test of our readiness for friendship occurs when
our companion outshines us. It can be in the form of achievement, winning the prize which we coveted; or through the
presenting of an idea or a scheme that finds more favour than
our own. Or through gaining the admiration or indeed the
love that we desperately longed for. Can we genuinely

rejoice at the success of one who is close and yet potentially a rival? Or do we use subtle measures to diffuse the glow that he is enjoying? Or to shift the scene abruptly to cut short the celebration? Or do we join heartily in the adulation, whilst secretly resenting the unfairness of fate? Can we enjoy one another when we are so vulnerable, so unsure of ourselves, so easily drowning in depression or feeling unappreciated and unloved?

Can we overcome all our deep-down conflicts and self-doubts, our hurts and shame, to reach out beyond ourselves to our fellows, to those who would be our companions?

Enjoyment is a matter of *joy,* and this is not easily defined or fathomed: again, it has to do with feeling, and so is not readily fixed in the definition. But we know what joy is, even if we cannot describe it in words: it is expressed in the sound 'Ah!' which comes from the heart.

But at times we have to use our heads and apply our minds to the question 'Can we enjoy one another?' or, more specifically, 'Can I enjoy you?' I may have to think hard about it, analysing the factors that affect our relating. There will be barriers in myself, due to my insecurity, my shadow and my darker self; above all due to my sense of inadequacy compared with you, and my fear that you will hurt me. Can we meet as Adult to Adult, or will you try to be Parent to the Child in me? Are you going to show me up?

Or else I may find you insignificant and somewhat irritating, even boring. I become anxious that it may affect my standing in the world, my reputation, if I am seen associating with you.

Such considerations show that we have not really met. There has been too little flow of feeling to open my heart towards you. Until that happens we will not cross even the outer boundaries. But if we do seek the opportunity to meet in openness and mutual regard, or at least to attempt it, then something will happen between us and we may recognize that we have the substance for building a relationship. Then the subtle dynamics, both positive and negative, will go into action, and the relationship will take on its own life.

But then, having allowed it to begin, I have to take my share of responsibility for nurturing it and for its wellbeing. It could be bordering on the sinful to foster a relationship and then to neglect it, even if the other one does just this. If I want to remain true to what I have called into being, I have to accept it as a responsibility; I could have avoided becoming involved in it. Once conceived the relationship has a right to its own existence and the fulfilment of its potential. When I engage in a relationship it takes on a life of its own: it commences a biography.

This has a spiritual dimension: a commitment to a relationship calls a spiritual entity to enter into the covenant. And there are consequences when such an entity is then given no sustenance and no support: the covenant needs to be honoured. A relationship that is allowed to go foul pollutes the atmosphere, also for others. So if for any reason the relationship cannot go on, it is important for this fact to be faced and the relationship dissolved with a ritual of some kind, a verbal agreement, a letter, a conversation, or a prayer.

If we would achieve this kind of discipline and consciousness in regard to the forming, celebrating and winding up of relationships, we would make an important step in the evolution of true individuality, and thereby move beyond this to conscious and caring interdependence. In past ages relationships were safeguarded by guiding powers of a spiritual kind. Then, as the evolution of earthly consciousness progressed, first by rulers who wielded authority over our private lives, then by the strength of social norms. Man has progressively released himself from these parameters and now stands free, able to relate as and where he feels best for himself.

As this freedom belongs to the evolution of our individual consciousness, it requires of us to become responsible for the way we relate: for such freedom implies that we have the power to make or break each other. We can hope that out of this age of individual freedom there will develop the age of brotherhood.

The stage of brotherly love, of Philadelphia, will have to be striven for, so as to turn our Earth into a cosmos of love. And every well-cared-for relationship is a seed for this new state of mankind. Hence the need to employ spiritual resources in the building of our togetherness: thoughtfulness, being considerate and aware, drawing on the gift of feeling and selfless love, and good will in the way we act.

Along this path we will grow in stature and in the favour of God and also man.

# 10. Forging bonds

We are now able to bring together the various factors that play into the working of relationships. We have surveyed six aspects of soul activity that can be controlled or guided to a limited extent. These six variable states of my soul meet the similar changeable states of the person I relate to. This makes for a creative but also precarious dynamic in all relating. My being able to relate successfully depends on my awareness of these six aspects in myself and in the other person, my acceptance of how he is and my own power to guide these aspects in my own soul. There is the need for continual adjustment to the variables in the other person, who may be only partially able to guide and control them. The six aspects are these:

1. How I am with myself. How much am I in touch and at peace with myself as an individual person? My mood, my tendency to introversion.
2. How open I am: the degree I am able and willing to engage in the building of a relationship with others. My trust in reaching out beyond myself.
3. The sexuality factor, which affects all relationships to some extent.
4. The flow of feeling and love: what is working as a spiritual energy to encourage interaction and bonding.
6. The degree to which outer circumstances facilitate or hinder the nurturing of my relationships.

6. The spiritual dimension: the extent to which deeper ideals and perceptions are shared and worked on together, and the degree of soul-intimacy which is allowed.

The modern world, Western model, begets broken relationships. Life moves fast, people are overfilled with information arising from the amazing advances of modern technology: time is sucked away by the Grey Gentlemen.[5] The need to concentrate intellectual and will forces, in order to keep up with demands, drives out the element of feeling. As a result, interrelating and co-operating with others can be draining and exhausting because there is no love, nor interest, and no time to regard one another with any kind of warmth.

We could try to roll all this back, and set out to build a healthy, cheerful community that enables people to live and work together purposefully and harmoniously. What would we need in order to guide ourselves towards togetherness with others? Here is a list as a sample:

## *What makes for success in relating?*
1. Inner freedom.
2. Readiness to address any problem that arises.
3. Honesty and congruence.
4. Courage to face knowns and unknowns, in what happens externally and also within us.
5. Trust in the process, even if it is sometimes uncomfortable.
6. Awareness that men and women are different in the constitution of their souls. We will explore this later.
7. A relationship benefits from all the six aspects indicated earlier in this chapter. If any one of them is

neglected or denied, the relationship will come under stress.

8. The track record of a relationship is worth examining, so that all that has taken place can yield its learning. Especially the difficulties. If these are examined together, the tough time can be recognized as a valuable part of the process, and thereby its hurts are healed and new energy is released.

9. Accepting change: Relationships are never static: the passing of time brings ever-new experiences. These keep relationships fresh, if they can be welcomed as part of the process of developing togetherness.

Relating is never without problems, and at times we have to go through discomfort zones, maybe resulting from problematic behaviour. Sometimes this stems from pathological states that would require therapy. But much of our behaviour is under our own control: we don't need to be insensitive in our attitude to others, or to make selfish demands on others without giving anything in return. Here is a suggested checklist. Would your own list be similar?

*Weaknesses in behaviour which affect relationships:*
Being — pedantic, fussy, stuck, opinionated, judgmental, banal, sarcastic, mocking, cynical, touchy, unforgiving, inconsiderate, heavy, snobbish.

Then come the more serious problems:
Being — depressive, brutal, insincere, dishonest, untruthful, scathing, destructive, driven by uncontrolled anger, subject to addiction (from alcohol to religion), insufferably proud,  insecure, gripped by hatred.

You can ask yourself: How is it with those people I associate with? <u>Do they have to put up with any of these tendencies in me</u>? And can I have the courage to realize that with effort these problems can be overcome, once I acknowledge them and decide to work on them?

# 11. It takes work to be social

Relationship-building asks for regular practice. The instrument of amiability needs careful tuning, and the player has to train basic skills in order to attain virtuosity. Life in our age of individualism does not incline us towards sociability; if anything it can generate a cynical distrust of others or a disparagement of ourselves.

The person who is content with his lot, and accepts it positively with good grace, is a balm to those around: already this is a social achievement. Personal contentment and enjoyment of life keep one fit for the fray of living with others.

All persons will have their own way of selecting their aims: it belongs to our individual philosophy of life. I share with you my own suggestions, but only as a stimulus for you to work the guide-lines that apply to you.

*To keep physically active.* The healthy person can more easily transcend himself and reach out to others in love or thought, and can be helpful in practical ways. Compare this with the person whose attention is focused on his own ailments and soul needs. Physical activity digests and dissolves unpleasant experiences and worries, and helps to engender a healthy transforming of depressive sentiments into plans of action. A daily walk in nature for half-an-hour is one prescription for remaining cheerful.

*To develop a sense for order.* What is the advantage of being a tidy person? The art of tidiness has to do with the completing of a task, including clearing up at the end of it.

An outer discipline in this respect will foster the inner one of not leaving unfinished business in one's soul. It is aesthetically feeding to live and work without the clutter of unpenetrated 'stuff.' But there is more to it than this. Reverence begins with small things: for instance the toothpaste tube in the bathroom. Anyone who works with children, and in particular children with a handicap, will know the importance of this 'devotion to small things': it helps the children to develop their basic trust. And in general life: careful wrapping of a present, removing a dead leaf on a pot plant, accurately laying a table for a meal, drawing up a job description, cleaning a car, all require devotion to detail.

*To have reverence for each other* is one of the virtues of social living. This goes without saying, but it does not go without doing. 'Devotion to small things' in all realms of life changes saying into doing, because the way we handle the small things affects each other all the time. Also the way we greet our partner in the morning, and welcome the children back from school. Indeed this reverence for things and events can apply to all of life.

*To develop a sense of what is important* in all aspects of the way one lives. There are many issues to address and evaluate. For instance: Is religion important? Why do people go to services? For their own benefit, or for the healing of mankind? Can we learn to think generously about such questions, respecting unconditionally what others uphold for themselves? How do we stand towards commitment? Does making a commitment sound like giving up freedom, or does it actually make one free?

*To think creatively.* Are you developing your right brain along with the left?[6] Are you allowing your creativity to have expression? Or is it being killed off by computers, traffic and other stresses? Do you see yourself as a creative person, open to inspiration and fresh ideas, but also willing to go through with the hard work needed to ground your visions? Or do you think like a calculator, accurately and instantly but never innovatively? There are basic tasks that require left brain; but life, contentment and reaching out call for the right brain to be enlivened. Being creative requires dedication. Our dedication commits us to the task in front of us, and calls up the energy we need to fuel our achievement. We allow ourselves to be a channel through which something original and true can enter the earthly world.

*To act in terms of the future.* What do you wish to achieve in the next five or ten years? Can you describe your main aim in life, and the goals you need to reach so as to get there? What will you leave behind you when you die: will it be an improved society, a contented family, something that you have made and that others can go on using, an organization that will continue without you and still prosper? To think about such questions will help you to become more clear about your own life, and your own clarity will make you more interesting to others. They will be drawn to you because you have something to give.

*To bear in mind constantly that our thoughts and feelings have an effect on our surroundings.* They make an impact. They can encourage or lame another person, promoting or retarding his impulses. A thought is like a pulse that vibrates in the ether: it can work as a blessing or cause pollution.

*To be reassured that we all count, as important members of the human community.* We have each come to earth with a mission, a task to fulfil. The mix of abilities and handicaps which are given to us is part of the plan; what we do with what we are endowed with is for us to determine. The divine element in each of us makes us infinitely valuable, so we carry a great responsibility for being adequate vehicles of that noble part. Noble we are, a nobleness we can distort or render invisible, or which can be so overlain with dross that no-one can see it. Yet our being human gives us this core of worth that no-one may deny, not even ourselves. Just as we should regard each other in a positive light, so too should we regard ourselves.

*To acquire the art of stillness in our souls.* Once we realize the cosmic importance of our being, we can nurture this God-within-us by tranquil contemplating of an idea, an object in nature, or a work of art. The cultivation of this inner stillness will engender peace in our souls. To begin with there could be anything but silence when we listen to ourselves, and to all that rises into consciousness from our memories, our anxieties, our longings, our impulses, our imagining of scenes past or future, our emotions: these could stir up the opposite of stillness. Yet all that comes up, unbidden, to cloud our consciousness just when we wanted space and peace within to contemplate something quite different, can be penetrated with our own thought-activity. If we accept the emotions and day-dreams, the worries and inner conflicts, asking them to reveal themselves fully to the penetrating analysis of our thinking, we can transform them into plans for action, or dissolve them as chimera. A way of doing this is to write a journal; and to describe the various promptings of our subconscious, and even of our conscious soul life. Writing requires thought and action, as well as dedication: this marshals the soul's forces. Inner stillness is a balance to our outgoing activity: it gives us the chance to rest, review and digest our experiences, and link again to the source of our inspiration. This state of soul will develop into the power to listen, a further necessary attribute of a social person.

It will also develop another attribute that belongs to a well-functioning person: *gratefulness.* Expressing our thanks means reaching out to others; it perfects the process of giving and receiving. It warms our thoughts, moving them from consciousness of head to the raying out of heart: the 'i' in thinking becomes the 'a' in thanking. Gratefulness also recognizes the less obvious acts of kindness and of sacrificing that come towards us continually, in crisis and in general life. A grateful person is an aware one, and every deed of gratitude is suffused with joy: it costs little and yet is of great worth. Thanking expresses love. Rudolf Steiner has written:

> Nothing can reveal itself to us which we do
> not love. And every revelation must fill us
> with thankfulness, for we ourselves are the
> richer for it.[7]

*To see all life's events as opportunities for learning.* We can question the essential purpose of our life on earth, and an answer can be 'to develop learning and giving.' The art of learning from life is to sift out from the mass of daily occurrences the message they contain for us. Even the rhythmical events of the cosmos have something to tell us, for instance the day-by-day rising of the sun. Here is an example of keeping going: the sun never gets tired, so we can say that the sun-centre in us, our heart, never gets tired. If we work out of our heart we can keep going, and be reinvigorated as we use our energy. That is something we can learn anew each day.

These ten aims amount to a suggested programme of self-discipline. There are doubtless many more aims that could spring to mind. The skills of relating need this kind of self-guidance: it is better to set these aims for oneself than to take over someone else's suggestions. So the ones presented above are only to set you thinking; your own list would reflect your own need and also your personal situation. And the items on your list could change as you progress.

# 12. Feeling

And so again to feeling. The motif of feeling comes frequently in these pages. Does our way of characterizing feeling begin to make sense? Can we see this as the distinguishing feature of the human being? It may be daring to ask this: thinking and willing obviously have a vital task within the human soul. But could it be that their ultimate task is to enable feeling to grow?

The element of feeling will be increasingly recognized as the bearer of love: true warm relating will become more and more natural, and the divine will unite with the earthly, giving new life to what was dying, and initiating a new cosmos. The rift between 'heaven' and 'earth' will be no more, and the creative words of Christ will lead mankind towards a new state of being. Life, joy and a sense of purpose belong to our new time: they will enter our world on the wings of a fine substance that we can already discern in the experience of pure feeling. This will be different from how it is now with most of us whose soul-experience is derived largely from emotions and bodily experiences. But we all have moments when we can experience such pure feeling: when we watch a sunset, see a noble deed, or survey a work of art that speaks to us.

Till now man's willing has depended on himself. This is set to change. He will derive his strength from the outpouring of divine love, which will reach him through the working of Christ in the flow of feeling. A sign of this happening will be a stirring of reverence, compassion and inner devotion in the human soul, lifting it out of its dependence on instincts and drives, and opening it towards a higher nobleness. Recognition of our true image brings us into harmony with ourselves, and makes it easier to relate to others.

There is in all this an unfolding of hope. We need this: for if we cannot see a brighter vision for the future of humanity, we succumb to despair at the enormous problems that mankind has to bear. For how can I be cheerful when so many are starving, suffering under dreadful poverty and oppression, or losing their sanity under the stress of modern life, or using violence and murder to achieve their aims? Must I renounce all happiness because of these problems? This is a cruel question: I can take in at least some information about these woes, but how can I help the tide to be rolled back?

There is a way. I can make a contribution towards strengthening the invisible forces that will be needed so as to overcome evil with good. I can make myself into a channel through which spiritual energy can work into the areas of life and levels of existence that need to be penetrated. Each of us is part of the very world we need to change, but we can each become a receiving-point for this higher influence. This higher influence is the power of Christ as He returns in glory 'in the clouds.' That means, in the forces that bestow life and provide the formative element in nature and in man.

The 'second coming' will be an individual experience of this creative power, filled with divine love, that will bring man to his new state. Every deed of love, every attempt at understanding each other and of working together in harmony, as shown to us by the co-operation of our two hands, helps to create an atmosphere that can absorb the light of the spirit and imbue our world with its energy.

All this could go wrong, because opposing forces are at work. Instead of the health-giving light of the spirit there could come a searing energy that would destroy the earth. As yet this lies locked up in sub-nature, but it could be released in a single blinding flash. The opposing forces work on man's pride and his lust for power: he *can* release such energies, and he is sorely tempted. We know how close we have been to such a catastrophe in our time.

The forces that would remove this danger are being prepared in human souls who strive to be bearers and conveyors of divine love. And this love can reveal itself in the way we relate to one another and bring about a mature, conscious and positive togetherness.

The obstacles to healthy togetherness are a reflection of our problematic present. The achievement of healthy togetherness, despite the obstacles, will help to create a harmonious future.

# 13. Not for myself

Could you define love? Could you describe it? It is both feminine and masculine, and the fusion of man and woman is called 'making love.' There are instincts that drive love, emotions that play with it, thoughts that try to guide it, commitments that consolidate it, conventions that either liberate it or bind it hand and foot. Civilizations have come and gone, structures in society have evolved, patterns of behaviour have changed. And love? In its essence love has always been itself, riding above the alterations that it found. Always a mystery, yet known in its power.

Power. This word can be used in a sense that denies freedom: but also to denote the potential that makes special acts possible; a force that is refined, positive and well-wishing. Love is a power that works through our souls. It comes from heaven and reminds us of our spiritual origin. It gives us the potential to fulfil our mission on earth. When we act out of love, even if it is difficult to do so, we know in our hearts that it is good. There is satisfaction, and the energy needed sustains itself. It is as if some other force is working in us, that does not spring out of our own soul. We are channels, instruments of a higher power: it flows with our feeling, engaging our thought and will in the process. It enables us to go beyond ourselves and reach out to our fellow human beings. Or to care for the world of nature or the objects that we use for our work or recreation, and for our sustenance.

When we love the world around us we can begin to know its secrets, its inner being. There can be openness to nature,

and to the plants and animals that belong to our life; there
can be affection for persons who feature in our lives, attachment to places or objects that are important to us. As we
mentioned in an earlier chapter, there is deep wisdom in
remembering that we cannot really know anything unless we
love it. The motif of love is 'not for myself.'

Yet we do have to make a distinction between love that
is pure and selfless, and various manifestations of a lesser
love that is intensely bound up with our own natural being.
Such is the love that is instinctive, that has to do with nurturing and protecting our own progeny: mother-love. A cat
will go again and again into a burning building to rescue
her kittens, regardless of her own safety. And a human
mother would do anything for her young children. A step
beyond this is the love that bonds a family or a tribe: this
love flows in the very blood that is inherited, and explains
the custom of avoiding marriage outside of one's own people. Very different is the state of falling in love, of finding
oneself in emotional dependency and elation towards
another person, usually of the other sex. Idyllic stories
abound, ending in lasting happiness or devastating disappointment. Romantic emotions outweigh the sober coun-
sels of reason and put those who fall in love at risk: but
whatever the outcome, bliss or broken heart, those who are
in love discover new dimensions in soul feeling.

Another form of love, based on a mixture of promptings,
is brotherly love: camaraderie, the team bonding, loyalty to
one's group, in the enthusiastic pursuit of a common goal. We
can describe it as *esprit de corps* or the rapture of sinking
one's individuality into a group. Yet all too often it is fuelled
by a blatant self-interest, however altruistic it may appear.
Indeed all forms of instinctive or emotional dedication can be
self-love in disguise. They spring from a poverty of soul
rather than a richness. Even mother-love can become restrict-

ing once the infant makes steps into childhood, not to mention adolescence: if the child's need for increasing independence is denied by a mother who wants him to remain dependent, her love degenerates into smother-love.

To aspire to be a channel of pure love a person has to be free. This is the love that is spiritual, based on truth and knowledge. With this love we move from personal self-centredness into the ability to embrace the whole of humanity and all of the universe. This is the power that brings harmony and joy wherever there is openness for its challenge. It calls up truth and integrity wherever it touches. People touched by this pure spiritual love will become aware of something that starts to change in themselves; they will develop the impulse to work on themselves to address their own weaknesses, and will reach out to others with compassion and understanding. This love will never condescend to help someone because he is needy. It will bind wounds and staunch the bleeding of those who suffer, because it recognizes them for their true humanity and not for their weakness. This love looks beyond personal failings, seeing only the infinite worth of individual human beings. It will never try to dominate, or seek to prevail or to be proved right. In its greatness it will want to serve, and no person and no creature would be deemed not worthy to be served.

A relationship based on this love will be founded in heaven for eternity. It will continue beyond the current lives of those it bonds: they will find their friendship deepening and maturing with the passing of time, and transcending death into the life to come.

This spiritual love, known in Greek as *agapé,* entered humanity through the Christ, although the way had been prepared by Buddha centuries before. Christ's incarnation in Jesus was God's gift to the Earth, which was fulfilled through Christ's sacrifice on Golgotha. This deed was a necessity for man. For without the introduction of spiritual love into the stream of mankind, the forces of selfishness would have proved victorious. As it is, the reversing of the trend has been effective to only a minor degree; but the nucleus has been implanted, and it will gain power once the struggle against materialism has been successful. Though only slowly, there is change happening in the world: empathy and caring are growing as mankind learns to face the consequences of injustice, greed and a denial of higher values.

We have touched on the affinity of peoples who were originally bonded through the blood. As tribal blood-purity was gradually diluted through intermarriage, so the unit of togetherness became smaller. Clans broke up into smaller groups, and the blood bond began to lose its power. What had been the egotism of the large group became the egotism of the small group and the family, and even this has been still further concentrated until we are seeing, in our time, the egotism of the individual. It had to go all this way. But with the coming of Christ, thanks to his uniting himself with mankind, a counterforce entered the stream of humanity. This force is spiritual love, a love that is free from egotism and is carried in the flow of human feeling. This is the love that says 'not for myself.'

The power of Christ works for all of humanity and is the spiritual counterpart of the Sun. Just as all plants are united in their dependence on the physical sun, so men and women on earth are united in their openness to the power of love, coming from the Spiritual Sun, the being of Christ.

There are those who acknowledge this being that stands behind the power of universal life: they are 'true Christians.' There are also other 'true Christians': their religion may not use this name, yet they too acknowledge a being who stands behind the power of universal life. They also strive to be pure channels for the flow of spiritual love into the world. It is the aim of this higher love to bring about a heavenly state on earth: for indeed a heavenly state would come about if all human beings would devote themselves to the cultivation of spiritual love in their daily lives.

In spite of all the risks, marriage offers the ideal opportunity to practise the virtue of spiritual love. For in marriage the partners can search together for the same truth, asking the same questions, even if they are at different stages of inner development. They can experience the elation and bliss of harmony and co-operation, and work out of a full regard for each other. They can strive to uphold the spiritual potential in each other. Their mutual loyalty and support enables them to delve deeply into each other's soul, bringing healing and a flow of life-energy where there are hurts and blocks, and releasing new forces. They will be clearly and warmly aware of each other's needs at all levels, and will seek to help wherever appropriate. Each will know when the other needs solitude to work out a problem alone, or has to seek help from outside the marriage; this would be supported in full trust. They would recognize each other's need, from time to time, to come to stillness and just be passive. They would find in themselves the energy and devotion to accompany each other through disappointment, illness and crisis. Yet each would remain a full, authentic, individual person.

——— o O o ———

The problem of the human being is based on the fact that instinct and emotion stir the self-indulgent longing for the physical sexual impulse, whereas the joining of forces of soul and spirit requires conscious effort, and the overcoming of self-centredness and self-indulgence.

It is also true that striving for spiritual enlightenment can have an egotistic motivation, giving rise to intellectual arrogance, domination of others, or the attempt to amass wealth for oneself. Misleading powers confront man on two sides. There are spiritual powers of a dark kind that influence human thinking with incredibly potent cleverness: their machinations have produced a technology devoid of anything heavenly or selfless. There are other fallen powers of an enticing kind that try to draw man's consciousness right away from the earth, to dwell in ideas and feelings that bemuse the soul and inflate it with haughtiness and superiority. Both these false powers can be distinguished from true spiritual powers, by applying the test 'Do they make a person more free or less free to be his true self?' True spiritual forces are inflexibly moral and will cease to fructify a soul that is riddled with egotism and uses spiritual energy for selfish ends.

We have mentioned three levels of love: *agapé, philia,* and *eros.* Usually these different depictions of love are seen as separate, only marginally overlapping with each other or sharing the same space. *Agapé* is the selfless spiritual love which has featured predominantly in our exploration; *philia,* the friendly warm feeling that enables people to get on well with each other, but stops short at self-sacrifice. *Eros* nowadays is drawn fully into the sexual, where indeed it has its place, because its stimulus comes from the other sex: but it does not really mean a blind desire for sexual action or a stimulation of sexual instinct; eros is more noble than this. The wanton succumbing to a drive to 'have sex' and to break through the parameters of acceptable behaviour can be called *hubris,* the Greek word for wanton behaviour. It implies violation, insolence and outrage, even grievous assault. 'Wantonness' conveys unrestrained behaviour, unchaste, licentious. By comparison *eros* is a cheerful god, and he brings out the delight a man can feel when stirred with enthusiasm and adoration generally for the beauty, grace and ineffable wonder of a woman.

So we have *agapé* as the ideal, *philia* and *eros* as the human, *hubris* as the sub-human. *Philia* and *eros* can be made sublime by the power of *agapé*. And this is the message to be heard: *philia* can be raised to *agapé* to the extent that selfishness is overcome; its warm fellow-feeling opens the way for the heavens to pour their elixir of pure love into the cups of friends rejoicing at their togetherness. And the madness of *eros,* its ecstasy, can become deep-felt respect and regard, free of selfish indulgence, when its song, dance and display of Dionysian energy become the bearers of true feeling, turning frenzy into enjoyment.

And even *hubris,* that seems a lost cause, can be transformed. For we can understand the division of the sexes as that which enables the individual to converse with the gods, and not as the excuse for debauchery, lust and violation.

Then a new culture could pervade the sphere of sexuality. It could arise in the spirit and work through the soul. It can then find a response in the human sexual body, enabling persons to know the energies and delights to be derived through their sexual natures; these they can then enjoy as worthily belonging to their humanity. Once *agapé* can pervade the realm of sexuality, the sting of evil is taken from it, for it becomes an expression of selflessness and fulfilment.

So the three levels of love are not compartmentalized: they can each contribute to human happiness and wellbeing, provided *agapé,* spiritual love, pervades the other two.

# 14. The way of love

Human love that is carried by the warmth of true feeling, and derives its energy from the spiritual dimension of our life, is an ideal form of love. Ideal both in the sense of something to aim at which will be difficult to achieve, and also in the platonic meaning of Idea, it enables us to penetrate into the depths of phenomena and to reach the creative and formative idea behind each phenomenon. It leads us towards intuition, the highest form of cognition.

As most of us have a long way to go before our soul becomes a bearer of this kind of love, we can take this as a challenge and strive towards it. We can see ourselves, together with the main part of humanity, as trying to purify and spiritualize our way of loving. This will take much time and the devotion of much soul-energy. It will call up in us a high degree of awareness of our actions and the will to transform our way of thinking. For what is required is that we perceive the eternal element in all persons and situations that we encounter in daily life. We can be comforted by the knowledge that our very ordinary daily experiences provide opportunities for growing in our awareness of the spiritual, the eternal, in all that is seemingly transient. The days go by, and if each day brings us one tiny step forward, we can indeed make progress. One day we stop to look at the view just round the corner: we suddenly notice its beauty for the first time. A stranger gives us his place in the queue, because he realizes we are in a hurry; it is good of him, and we are grateful. We are offended when a neighbour contradicts us about something we know quite well: but for once we really listen to her and recognize that her side of the story is just as valid as our own. Small steps each time, yet they lead us onward. We can look back after a year and notice that we have grown in the clarity and depth of our soul life.

At night, when we meet our true Self in sleep, we digest our experiences and review their meaning. Once we have set our aims, our true Self can sift what is relevant from the happenings of the day. So nothing is lost in our daily experience: all is evaluated, and the Self absorbs the good yield. On waking up the next morning, we lose our awareness of this, but we are nearer to achieving our aim.

An aim to develop spiritual love will gradually open the channels through which this love can flow; if we look for the eternal being in everyone, we will find that this reveals itself more and more in those we meet or turn to in our thoughts. And our thoughts themselves will gradually become free: free from the pressures of our instincts and emotions, our memories and our subconscious longings. Thereby the basic conditions for the growth of spiritual love will be met. We will become bearers of a power of feeling that carries warmth of regard and thankfulness to our surroundings. We will develop selfless love.

A picture of the transformation that this process will bring about is the change that takes place at dawn after a moonlit night. As the cool, silvery light of the moon becomes less strong, a new colourful brightness arises in the east, heralding the golden sun. The moment comes when the new light of day pierces the horizon and permeates all spaces that are open to it with its warm light. In regions where summers are hot and dry, the first rains are like a grace bestowed upon nature: all plant life is refreshed and renewed, and the soil revives its chemistry. In regions that are snow-bound all winter, the first sight of green grass brings a similar joy.

Without sun and rain there could be no life on earth. But man needs more than this. Without spiritual love we lose our humanity. The seven sacraments of the Christian life signify the outpouring of spiritual love into the souls of human beings, as they progress through the stages and rhythms of their life:

— Baptism helps the soul to incarnate and take hold of the new body.

— Confirmation strengthens the soul life of the adolescent person, so that the Self can begin to take hold of its bearer.

— The Communion Service consecrates the person and enables Christ-power to permeate the soul and overcome its separation from heavenly forces.

— The personal Consultation (originally called Confession) helps the individual person to recognize himself as growing and learning, and so releases his love for God and for his fellow man.

— Marriage forges a higher unity between a man and a woman, blessing their intention towards togetherness.

— Ordination recognizes that in all persons there is a potential priest and that the layman is also called to enter the mysteries that lead human development towards the spirit.

— Anointing prepares the person for his return to the full consciousness of the Spirit.

In these seven archetypal ways the spiritual world comes close to mankind on earth. They are all deeds of love which can call up in each of us an impulse to help each other to be recognized and to develop as a full human being. As spiritual love is our theme we can recognize that the Sacraments testify to the love of the spirit for all persons who are on earth, as they work through their destinies and strive to fulfil their missions. These seven ways can be summed up as follows. We can hear them first of all as the voice of the spiritual world addressing us. And then, as each of these ways becomes our own, we will be able to speak the words ourselves, conveying the same blessing to those around us:

— I help you to be yourself.
— I recognize you as a person who is growing.
— I wish for you to be open to the eternal in yourself and to be healed from selfishness which cuts you off from the spirit.
— I call on you to connect your way of thinking to the eternal, and to allow love to arise in you as a response.
— I bless you in companionship, that you may inspire and assist each other in a bonding that is watched over by a spiritual being.
— I see the priest in you, which can transform the earth into a cosmos of love.
— I help you on your way to your spiritual home.

We do not change another person through spiritual love: we help him to be free to be himself. We strive to create a safe space for him to fill, large enough to enable him to grow, yet firm enough to assure him of our understanding and our regard for him. We will not intrude with advice unless it is asked for, and even then we will encourage him to find his own solutions. We will not cross his boundaries and invade his space; we are not allowed to force him to be free. We will only seek to transform the moonlight of his aloneness into the sunlight of companionship.

Our love will help him to be free in so far as it comes from our own inner freedom.

This calls for tact and self-knowledge, and also caring devotion. It requires of us to strive for selflessness.

The way of love encourages us:
— to develop a kind of thinking that takes in the eternal, spiritual dimension;
— to ensure that this thinking, originating in the head, expresses itself through the heart, safeguarding it from all forms of negative criticism;
— to be able to hold at bay the instincts and emotions: they can be seen, felt and recognized, but should not dictate our deeds and attitudes;
— to cultivate our ability to see or sense the idea behind all that we meet around us: this means judging our surroundings objectively, without either resisting what comes towards us or being swayed by it;
— to act morally: a way of testing the morality of one's intentions is to ask oneself 'would this be done in heaven?' Like this we take up the familiar words 'On earth, as it is in heaven.'
— to be willing to change our attitudes, judgments and patterns of thought, to accord with the ever-new situations around us, and to give ourselves space to grow.

Love is joyful, but it can open the way to much suffering. Love implies commitment to those whom one loves, which can mean supporting them through hard times and bearing their grief. So love is joy and suffering.

Love is fragile. In oneself the spiritual love may change into sensual love and become self-indulgent. Indeed it is an almost superhuman challenge to prevent this from happening. The only way is to accept the arousing of a desire for personal enjoyment whilst remaining aware of what is happening. Love is to be enjoyed, but once it is taken up in the emotions it becomes subject to these mood-swings. This makes it fragile. Moreover, the person whom one loves in this ambivalent way, ideally and sensually at the same time, may become confused by the double signal.

*Eros* is delightful but *eris* can be devastating. A small step from the one to the other! *Eris* is the Greek word for strife and quarrel, contention and rivalry. As soon as *eros* is crossed or balked, an emotional charge spells out 'fight or flight': and if fight wins, the change to *eris* sets in. It has been said that love and conflict go together. But again, this love is not *agapé:* it would make all the difference if it would be *agapé,* which would remain sovereign in the face of such a challenge. Until we can aspire to spiritual love we have to reckon with a good deal of turbulence in our relationships: there is only a thin line between love and anger.

And, finally, we have to remember that none of us is free of *hubris,* of wantonness, even though it may be well disguised. In the past, society imposed rules of good manners to keep *hubris* at bay; but these rules are less acceptable in our time, so each person is left to tame this wolf within himself or the hyena within herself.

So the way to love is fraught with many challenges and pitfalls. The one who would love selflessly, truly and with grace has to be master over his or her self; his true Ego needs to gain sovereignty over the lower ego, and to guide him to enjoy togetherness with others, in such a way that integrity is not lost. Integrity is a key word: it covers wholeness, uprightness and honesty.

A step towards achieving this is to come to peace with oneself. The person who accepts himself or herself, with all the weakness and unfulfilled longing, insecurity and inadequacy that belongs to one, is nevertheless able to respond to the beauty and also the need presented by others. A person who is well-centred will not be self-centred.

A second step towards integrity and sovereignty is to be able to distinguish between the eternal and the ephemeral.

A third is the ability to communicate.

And a fourth has to do with being aware of boundaries that are either never to be crossed, or that can only be crossed by agreement with the other.

A fifth is to honour agreements.

# 15. Exploring the feminine

This study of relationship brings us to a new vista. The nature and quality of relationship has changed a great deal in the course of the current century, and is set to change all the more as we enter the new millennium. Recent years have been dramatic; the frontier has moved.

Where are advanced young people now? One thing is clear: they have freed themselves from the stereotype of 'man' and 'woman.' The way they feel and act is no longer determined by their gender. In caring and nurturing a man is becoming equal to a woman. And a woman can command respect for her leadership, determination and logical thinking. We can no longer compare the contrasting qualities and tendencies that belong to men and to women: the roles are becoming increasingly interchangeable. And so are the soul qualities. Provided ...

Provided modern people have evolving within them both male and female principles. Each human being of today (and this will become more so in the future) manifests both principles: they are nowadays less and less related to gender.

This signifies a major change in the way human beings are endowed and how they live their lives. Deeply satisfying relationships grow between people as persons, regardless of gender. There are many same-sex relationships of love and friendship: and the demand is spreading for a recognition of commitment, also of legal marriage, with a person of the same sex.

Children, even if adopted, can feel secure in such 'families,' as many partnerships of this kind are as functional as the best of those between people of the opposite sex. The paradigm of father-role/male, mother-role/female is no longer the only way of establishing families.

Today we come across many situations of this kind, and we realize that new forces are at work, calling on us to think more widely about the state and development of the human being. We are in a time of transition which asks for a new openness and understanding. We have to go beyond the obvious and hitherto-accepted way of regarding woman and man in their lives and conduct.

So we have to be careful in fixing images in relation to men and women. We need to observe and examine the polarities in the human psyche, recognizing that gender is not always the determining factor in these polarities. There is working in modern persons a solvent that reduces the connection between gender and characteristics. This has both a negative and a positive effect. It causes rejection of anything that smacks of stereotyping, and condemns the perpetuation of roles associated with gender. At the same time it strives towards the achievement of wholeness in a human person, in which the feminine and masculine traits both have their influence on the personality and acumen.

## Persons

The very word *person* conjures up a picture of wholeness: all human qualities can vest in a 'person.' And more than this. The concept 'person' indicates that something sounds through: *per-sonare*. But what sounds through can be of a divine nature or come from the realm of the demons: and so persons need to be conscious of what sounds through them, and to distinguish the good from the evil, the angel from the beast. Discrimination becomes essential: the person has to take full responsibility for what is said, thought or done.

The female principle seeks to give support and love to fellow human beings. Whereas the male principle in each person observes, initiates, directs and adjusts, and (ideally) does so with the minimum of emotion: it acts *cerebrally* (from the left-hemisphere). The male principle is essentially goal-directed, and it can only achieve if it is free to absorb itself in the current task.

The feminine is closer to the spirit than the masculine; through it the universal becomes personal, the spiritual is humanized. Whereas the male principle strives to make the universal practical and bring the spiritual into everyday use.

## Differences

Without separateness there could be no relating. We can rejoice at the wisdom that made us all so different and therefore so essential as counterparts for each other. Life is constantly asking us to balance each other's one-sidedness, but also to respect each other's stage of development. Basically there are three groups of people.

Those who are so deeply steeped in the characteristics of their gender that they are scarcely aware of the transition that has affected western civilization in the last decades. They are mainly found in more conservative communities.

Those to whom the opening paragraphs of this chapter apply. They are the ones in whom the male and female principles are well-balanced and gender plays a role only in regard to child-begetting and childbearing. These are the ones who have been 'liberated' through recent trends in the western way of life.

And an in-between category who are still largely influenced by their gender. With these it is still relevant to speak of the difference between the attitudes and behaviour of men and women, showing how both display their typical strengths and weaknesses, although we also find men who are strong in the female principle, and women in the male.

The rest of this chapter and the next chapter apply to this third category: therefore it seems valid in this context to use the terms 'women' and 'men' in describing the way in which they are different. Those in the second category may find such distinctions irrelevant or even obnoxious, but yet helpful in seeking to understand acquaintances who are not fully emancipated from the effects of their own gender.

## The yin/yang that was

Women and men used to be seen as forming two halves of a whole. Today both are asserting their independent wholeness, women even more significantly than men. Within this climate marriage cannot remain the same: it has no place in the modern world unless it honours the equal worth of men and women. The old patterns of rules and duties no longer apply: the division of functions needs to be negotiated and agreed mutually, and nothing should be deemed to belong to the one or the other partner merely on the basis of gender. The partners in a modern marriage are thereby induced to respect and support each other's growth to wholeness.

## *Two contrasts*

Two propositions may be worth considering, to see whether you can support them out of your own experience. The first takes up the observation that for women healthy relating is paramount.

> The woman can work if her relationships are in good order, especially her relationship with a male partner. If this primary relationship is disturbed, her willpower is undermined; when it goes well, she can work enthusiastically and with abundant energy, even if the work is dull and repetitive. The man, on the other hand, needs first to have his work-life in order, and then he can relate. As soon as his work-life becomes a problem, he withdraws and finds it difficult to relate, especially to his female partner. So, for a woman, relationship is basic and joy in her work depends on it. And, for a man, the work comes first: and if this succeeds, relating comes about as a by-product.

It can often happen that a woman feels insecure and unloved, ignored and in the way, when her partner is stressed by a problem in his work. He does not mean to be unkind or inconsiderate; he is just preoccupied: his world seems to be falling apart. He *has* to withdraw and see to it, and he wants to do it himself. But a woman can't always understand this; she sees his plight and wants to reach out to help him. She does not realize that, rather than empowering him, she is thereby making him all the more conscious of his inadequacy. The worst she can do is to offer unbidden advice such as: 'Why don't you go and ask Jack? He is good at these things.!'

The other proposition for you to consider, and test with your observation, is this:

> The basic emotion, or ultimate driving force, in
> a woman is anger, and that in a man is fear.

This is controversial, but worth examining. A girl in mid-teens is likely to be outgoing, rebellious and full of strong opinions, whilst a mid-teen boy tends to be sensitive, diffident and easily withdraws. And the basic pattern is likely to continue into adulthood. If a conflict arises between a woman and a man, the woman may at first weep and be somewhat willowy, whilst the man is all out to stand his ground; but when it comes to fight or flight, see how the woman fights and the man seeks flight: it is the woman who is likely to go into verbal attack, while the man seeks a bolt hole in order to retreat. Even if he resorts to battering her, he shows his cowardice and thereby reveals his fear.

This view would explain why girls are brought up to be nicely behaved and boys are expected to be daring and play rough games. And men have to remember 'big boys don't cry'; they are encouraged to avoid showing their feelings. But women aroused have passionate strength and can be righteous in their wrath: this belongs to their approach to life and thereby also to their partnership. They see the ideal in a man and are angered whenever he fails to live up to this ideal. They spurn duplicity, dishonesty and lack of integrity. They may long to have an affair with another man, but they think of his wife and cannot bring themselves to hurt her. They fight for what they consider to be basic decency.

It is not only the flouting of decency that angers a woman. The phenomenon of anger as a basic drive in a woman is depicted in Marilyn French's novel *The Woman's Room*[8] and is the theme of Harriet Lerner's *The Dance of Anger.*[9] Dr Lerner describes the role of anger in the lives of women, and calls it a signal — one worth listening to — as a message that:

— the woman is failing to address an important emotional issue in her life;
— she is being hurt;
— her rights are being violated, or her needs or wishes are not being adequately met;
— her values are being compromised, possibly in a relationship, or her desires or ambitions are being balked;
— maybe she is giving or doing more than she can really manage;
— or others are doing too much for her and not enabling her to show her competence and grow;

Women have long been discouraged from the forthright expression of anger. Any woman who openly expresses anger at men is branded as unfeminine, unattractive, or even strident and a shrew! But deep down there is a noble energy being kindled into a roaring fire. This explains why women have great powers of endurance, and of love: for anger is close to love. Their anger is ignited by disappointment: 'Why do you let yourself down? I see the greatness in you, and you deny your own worth. Why? Why!'

# Integrity

A deep-going difference between women and men is shown by this. In their soul-life women are naturally one; they create a unity in body, soul and spirit. Different as these three entities are, the woman integrates them: the soul is the connecting link. Her soul-feeling unites with spirit-inspiration to give her intuitive insight; her soul-mood affects the body, soul-joy giving it buoyancy, soul-pain expressing itself in gestures of alarm, shock and distress.

A man's consciousness of spirit, soul and body does not have this natural integrity: he has to acquire it. And without this a man can embrace an ideal but let his soul be gripped by conflicting instincts and desires. He can bear bodily pain with a stiff upper lip and literally become detached from it. A woman is pained by the lack of this kind of integrity in a man. For her, integrity means moral integrity: and she herself wishes to be seen and recognized as a whole person, as wholesome, as integrated, as having integrity. It is distressing for her if her partner fails to recognize this.

When a woman finds her own fulfilment in a man, she gives a part of herself to him: she identifies the masculine element in her soul with him. She is then bonded. If the relationship enters the physical-sexual sphere, it is not only her body that she offers, but with it her soul and spirit. Thereby the bonding takes the risk of being turned into bondage. But she accepts this as wholesome provided the man she loves remains devoted to her; she allows herself to be vulnerable.

And she expects his loyalty towards her to be equally total and unwavering. If he divides his attention between her and another woman, she is deeply wounded. Because what she has given to him cannot be retrieved; it has been given without reserve, in total trust. His behaviour may seem to himself quite natural, for his interest in the other woman comes out of another compartment of his soul. He isn't aware that he is being disloyal: he just wants to gain a new experience that could enrich his soul and make his life more interesting. And he assures himself that this second liaison bears no commitment. But his view of the situation is generally not acceptable: it lacks integrity. The man may call his partner jealous, possessive and unreasonable: but a woman, who works out of her own integrity, wants to experience, admire, love and devote herself to the integrity of her man. She sees his oneness from the standpoint of her own oneness, and is hurt by his failure to live up to it himself. And she is worried by the threat to their oneness together.

When a woman makes love, her need and her soul-tendency is to devote herself with her whole being. Not to do so would prevent her from feeling fulfilled, and she would lose the desire for the relationship. A man easily 'makes love' with his body only, even when he loves his partner dearly. Men have to learn to love in wholeness, so as to be worthy of the love of a woman. This is a man's schooling in integration. When he fails, the woman suffers greatly.

## Not always easy

The life of a woman who is strongly identified with her gender is often far from easy, due to many factors. The transition of our societies to a less role-based culture will change this in radical ways, but until this happens there are areas that should be re-shaped and patterns changed. For often we find that the woman:

— has to bear the pressures of an overload of roles (career, family, household, social, professional);

— cannot devote herself fully to a career without renouncing some of the claims of motherhood;

— seldom has enough opportunity for cultural pursuits, on top of being an earner and a home-maker, and dealing with a host of menial tasks that use up her time and energy;

— has a dysfunctional marital relationship or one that has broken;

— experiences deep loneliness even when nurturing a family.

## *The ultimate difference*

The bearing of children brings a woman's soul to depths that are not attainable in men. No other experience can compare with that of motherhood, with its pain and joy. The fact that all women have this potential gives their inner life the quality that touches the eternal. In her soul life a woman transcends the earthly state; an inward force that dwells within the feminine opens the way to sensing the world of truth, beauty and goodness that exists beyond our everyday world. Life on earth makes its continual demands on her strength: but she is sustained by the knowledge that the other state can be reached in moments of true feeling. This knowledge gives contentment. She can be angry at the deceit, stupidity and moral weakness that she encounters every day, but in inner solitude she can let her thoughts and feelings enter this other world where the values she upholds are sovereign.

# 16. On being a man

We need to explore further the proposition in the previous chapter that the basic instinctive emotion in a man is fear. What makes it so?

There is in him a fear of not achieving, of not managing, of being inadequate. We have already mentioned the imp attached to his psyche, which sits on his left shoulder and says to him repeatedly 'Look at yourself! You're not doing very well, are you?' This wretched creature does its best to undermine his self-confidence, though it may succeed in spurring him on to prove it wrong. It is important for a man to achieve.

What must he achieve? To make a difference to his surrounding, to hold his own with his colleagues, to satisfy his own ambitions and reach the goals he has set himself. He may wish to impress his superiors, or his juniors, and the woman in his life; but the main person he has to satisfy is himself. He loves to watch how others manage, especially how the individuals work in a team: that is why he enjoys watching sport. In his dreams he is the star that goes with the team, then in a spurt of brilliant action breaks out, runs like lightning and ... scores. The vignette on the sports field is a symbol of his own wished-for victorious thrust to win. Then can come the joyful relaxing of tension, the cheering, the sense of having done it. The imp on his shoulder will be silenced, jolly well.

But never mention this secret fear. He has no defence except to resort to bravado, machismo, or just sheer denial. It is man's Achilles heel, and it makes him vulnerable.

How different from the vulnerability of a woman. For her, the flow of feeling is precious, true and loving: and when this is not received, often because it is taken as sentimentality, the woman suffers. A man suffers when any remark or event stirs the imp to scathing laughter and fires his snide remarks.

A man is often faced with the choice of fight-or-flight: as we observed in the last chapter, he is not a good match for the fury of a woman. But alongside or against other men, his yearning to prove himself will spur him on to fight: hence his frequent involvement in competition, debate, argument, eloquence, and ultimately violence. This is mainly with other men. He can of course resort to all these with women, but in doing so will possibly never come out the winner, however well he performs. For generally his performance has no effect on the woman's own conviction that she holds the moral high-ground.

The mention of violence brings up the tragic spectacle of the times we live in. There is a rising tide of violence in our present-day world; and the main perpetrators are men. The violence is often cowardly, crazy and self-destructing; yet it causes wave upon wave of misery and terror. Is it a coincidence that this phenomenon becomes a major threat just when women have achieved a greater degree of freedom and self-determination? Or is there a hidden connection? Could it be that woman's gain is man's loss, in so far as he can no longer fall back on his accustomed source of affirmation?

Another observation made in the last chapter had to do with the compartmentalization of a man's soul attitudes. He can be inspired and think in a spiritual way: indeed philosophers throughout history have mostly been men. And yet his daily life can deviate substantially from his professed ideals.

In the pragmatic interplay with others, with colleagues or with rivals, he can resort to methods that betray the lower instincts of envy and revenge. Or he can be strictly disciplined in his thinking and slovenly in his daily habits. He can write theses on social polity and be totally anti-social in his home; he can be a real chum to his pals and beastly to his wife. Such contradictions in his behaviour could indicate a resistance to facing himself. He is reluctant to go for psychotherapy, and in particular to marital counselling: the fear of being shown up goes deep. 'I know my problem ... up to a point ... and I don't need you to rub it into me.'

—— o O o ——

So much for the weaker side of a man. The changing consciousness in both women and men in our time means that a good deal is also happening to men: and there is hope that their weakness, their basic *angst,* will be transformed into a sensitive search for new values, based no longer on self-assertion and the desire to be effective and powerful.

The gulf between men and women becomes narrower. This does not imply that they are becoming 'effeminate,' but a gentle caring side of their otherwise masculine nature is emerging. They may still be coming from Mars (as Dr John Gray indicates in his popular book *Men are from Mars, Women are from Venus),*but Mars is changing.[10]

Let us make an excursion into modern (Western) spiritual science, for which we have to thank Rudolf Steiner. According to this knowledge, John Gray is on the way to being correct. Men do not come from Mars but do go through Mars on their earthbound journey of incarnation. This is the sphere where they take up qualities of courage and strength, characterized by the Mars metal of iron. Women also go through Mars, just as men also go through Venus; but the male incarnation displays these influences more strongly, just as the female displays the Venus qualities.

Man's reliance on fighting, which has dominated the pattern of human history through the ages, was set to change nearly four hundred years ago, at the hand of a major spiritual event. We are touching on ages of evolution, and such events take time to affect soul-behaviour. The change is pinpointed to the year 1604, when Christ, as the ruler of the Cosmos and the guide for mankind's development, gave a special task to the being we call Buddha. This being had incarnated as Siddhartha Gautama six centuries before Christ, to fulfil his mission of bringing to earth the qualities of compassion, love and awareness of the spirit. The new mission of Buddha was to go to Mars and transform its energies from aggression to compassionate caring. The Mars here referred to is not the visible red planet but the spiritual sphere of the heavens indicated by its orbit.

The effect of Buddha's influence is to bring about the transforming of aggressiveness into reaching out in love: the use of violence is to change into the practice of understanding. This change in the make-up of the man will gradually come about, and already the signs are to be seen. We more often meet men who are caring, open, and in touch with their feelings. We now find such qualities in men as well as women.

Such a major change will take time. However, the fore-runners have been around for a number of generations already: for instance the amazing 'brotherhood' of persons born with Down's Syndrome. They display a warmth of heart and a lack of aggression that has brought a new element into our midst. They are looked upon as 'retarded': and so modern medicine, able to recognize them during pregnancy by means of amniocentesis, turns readily to abortion in order to eradicate them. But modern medicine doesn't notice that they have appeared mainly in advanced 'Western' countries, where the element of love and warmth is at risk through the hectic pace of life connected with technology and materialism.

The transition from the strong, warlike man of old to the all-round caring man of the future is far from easy. The present-day tendency towards violence is a remnant of the old Mars influence, showing that the kinder, milder traits have not yet become widespread. But the constant search for peaceful solutions in international affairs, and the increasing pursuit of conflict resolution and reconciliation, contain the seeds of a more compassionate future.

Many of the men born during the decade that followed the end of the Second World War, in the western countries, brought with them a strong impulse to overcome the aggressive macho stance. But, as often happens, there were those who turned a noble intention into an aberration. The 'flower-people' were gentle, even soft, wanting to get away from the hardness of the earth and its constricting necessities. But they drained away their will-power in dreams, and resorted to psychedelic drugs to expand their consciousness and reach the Unseen. Their motto 'make love, not war' was in line with the spirit of the 'new Martians,' imbued with gentle compassion. But they lost all form, and could not take up or solve the problems of the time: they could only opt out.

There are those who have not chosen the illusory way to greater wholeness. They match the reality of our present world-situation with a new perception of the Spirit, and they devote themselves to healing work, art, education, the building of free intentional communities, a renewal of religion, and a re-enlivening of agriculture and architecture. They are striving to turn economic life away from competition, towards co-operation. They have set out to transform

the old ways of top-down authority into new forms of asso-
ciation and shared or revolving leadership. They seek a
path of inner development free of the constricting demands
of a guru and based on slow but steady devotion to inner
exercises.

They find themselves in harmony with the universal wisdom that has been taught through the ages: they recognize
that modern man can also reach the truth through clear imaginative thinking. And in the same way modern man can also
intuit the good, and thereby morality can cease to be a code
prescribed by outer authority, and become a guiding force
within each person, making him free, authentic and responsible.

This new direction for mankind is backed by a vast
body of knowledge that can be examined and tested by
individuals using the appropriate methods. This new science of the spirit combines with an insight into the being
of Man, giving modern persons a stimulus to transcend
their fears and frustrations and work positively towards a
civilization in which men and women will see the true
being in each other. They will know how to unite their
efforts in creating a new pattern for social living, in which
society respects individual as much as individual respects
society. This ideal is still a long way off, but the means are
there to attain it, and there are many who are engaged in
this endeavour.

In all this the man can do his work, knowing deep
down that he has the potential to be a full human person,
with emerging feminine qualities that widen and warm
his masculine being, healing his one-sidedness and making
him a good companion to men and to women. There is hope.

———— o O o ————

Yet we still have to try to understand the basic fear in a man today. It is a feature of man in transition, and all transitions are scary. There is a complex of worries that each man has to encounter, welling up from within his soul, indeed coming up from a deep, generally unfathomable level in his subconscious being. Modern conditions make it more difficult for a man to cope than used to be the case before the movement for the liberation of women got under way, and when the position of men in all spheres of life was more secure. Also before the change in the influence of Mars began: a transition that has only shown its effects in the last few decades.

A man has basic needs, which link up with his basic soul drives. He needs to be needed. His masculinity expresses itself in giving powerfully of his own quintessence. In our modern explicit culture we can call this the power of the penis. This is both the instrument and the symbol of potency which enables him to be dominant. Yet he is embarrassed and ashamed of this part of his make-up. It is not for display. This happened to Adam (and correspondingly to Eve) when they ate the apple: self-consciousness overwhelmed them — they felt the awakening of a force that needed to become private.

While the organ of masculinity is external, man has internalized his feeling for it. This paradox makes a man uneasy with himself, especially with his body, and this makes him vulnerable *per se*. So on the one hand the penis is the sign of power, on the other the source of self-conscious unsureness. He has the brute and the weakling interacting within his psyche. He is expected to 'be a man,' to prove his potency. And there gnaws at him the fear of impotence. He wants to be strong, but fears exposing his weakness. He relishes the admiration of others, but fears their ridicule. If his worries are not engendered by persons outside of himself, there is always the imp on his shoulder ready to get at him.

And all this alongside the emancipation of women: their liberation has increased their demands upon men; the pill has made them free. It has also removed the need for men to be more cautious and considerate. And more recently the fear of AIDS has come into the foreground: whilst contraception is designed to prevent life, the precautions against AIDS have to do with preventing death. The inner dynamics that beset a man have become more complex and more confusing through the recent decades.

The crisis in male identity is all the more deep-going because men have to take women into account: men in the not so distant past had mainly to make their agreements, their social contracts, with men. Now they have to include women fully: it is no longer a man's world. Rosalind Miles in her penetrating book *The Rites of Man* writes:

> For the dislocated man, 'Woman' (like 'Reds' or 'faggots' in times past) constitutes a shorthand for an uneasy sense of a profound, almost indescribable and certainly irreversible social change.
>
> 'Masculinity' has always been essentially a contract between men and men. As sub-contractors, however, women were vital to the scheme of things. But over the last twenty years or so, women have had their own contracts to reconsider and redraw, and suddenly all the old deals are off. A decade or two of feminism has not only changed the world for women: it has produced a crisis of response for the thinking man. How in this brave new post-patriarchal world is he to 'be a man' when all the time-dishonoured props, scripts, prerogatives and perks have been abolished or swept away?[11]

It is a fact that men in general are more vulnerable to suicide than women, and in all western cultures the young men in the fifteen to twenty-five age-group are most at risk. This shows that the entry into adulthood presents serious challenges to many. As Miles writes:

> Masculinity, it seems, has never been more fragile, even as it has never been more demanding, more potent, more exorbitant (p.11.).

One worrying aspect of the crisis in male identity is the large number of single-parent families. Children grow up without the natural presence of a father. For boys the absence of a regular role model as part of family life means the loss of a formative influence which he needs for the firming up of his personality. When the family life is weak or one-sided, young children cannot easily build up the basic trust that gives them a secure foundation for their lives.

Another concern that eats away at the sense of belonging and of being needed in young men is the serious lack of job-opportunities for those entering the employment market. To go through schooling and possibly tertiary education without much hope of getting a job is devastating to one's self-esteem.

Then comes the inevitable life-crisis as a man grows older: the mid-life crisis at around thirty-five to forty years, and the crisis of middle age between forty-five and fifty-five. In both there can be a challenge to a man's security in himself and in society.

Whilst we can take note of the precariousness of the male, we can hope that the present-day process of transition will lead men to a new self-confidence. A man has twelve positive roles, and in achieving them he proves his potential:

Man remains the giver of life, and so should not cause death through violence.

He can achieve the fulfilment of woman, not her subordination.

He can foster social co-operation, in place of competitiveness.

He can be a creative and imaginative thinker, and not merely a reactor or a calculator.

He can create wealth for the good of mankind, and not only for his own aggrandizement.

He can work the earth, enriching it instead of exploiting it.

He can be a king in the modern sense, not as ruler but as bearer of the destiny of his people (just as Christ showed the way by washing the feet of His disciples).

He can be a priest calling down blessings from heaven instead of trying to be a magician.

He can learn to be a lover, not one who demands love but can only give it to himself.

He can be a true husband, caring for the safety of the home, enabling the wife and the children to be secure and feel cherished.

He can be a father who stands by the mother and accompanies the children into their adulthood.

He can be one who grows in stature as a human being, who does not give up in the face of adversity, and who thereby provides a role-model for his family.

If he accepts these twelve points as aims to strive for, a man can learn the joy of serving and loving. He has to be able to accept failure and not succumb to the fear that he is not good enough. Fear saps self-confidence and can make him uncaring. The power of love, once it comes to life in him, will dissolve his tendency to be concerned primarily with himself: he will then want to help others to win.

# 17. Confiding

How wonderful it is when two persons have confidence in each other, and feel they can confide deeply in total security.

This is relating of the best kind; there is openness, a sense of freedom, trust and intimacy. Yet such confidence doesn't come as a free gift: it is only reached as the result of a process. Getting to know each other deeply implies recognizing each other's strengths and weaknesses, as we do with the people we meet around us every day. But now recognition must lead to acceptance: neither partner must feel inadequate, threatened or disempowered. Neither would wish to be 'one up' on the other, and there would be no hidden agenda, manipulation or any trace of disdain. 'I see you, and I cherish and support you fully. My regard for you is positive and unconditional.'

There must be rejoicing in heaven when such a relationship exists on earth: it is food for the gods. For if human beings come to this, it means they have cleared much clutter from their souls and have overcome the laming effects of pride, fear, anger, jealousy, suspicion and mistrust. When two or more people are truly together, a channel is open and something immortal can enter. And when two are together in the name of confiding love, a spiritual being can come and dwell in this space.

Here we touch on a vital aspect of modern spiritual knowledge: when a bond grows between two people, and is firmly established in total confidence, a spiritual entity, an angel, draws near: and this angel is then able to bring heavenly blessing into the midst of humanity through the vibrant space formed by that good relationship. It follows that a bonding of this quality not only benefits the ones in that relationship: it also brings a blessing into the wider social environment. Moreover, we can dare to add that all 'living' creatures, the elemental beings, the nature spirits and all the inhabitants of the heavens are warmed and nourished when two persons relate in true confidence.

The substance of trust is born with a baby: yet in the first years of life that trust can be destroyed. It then takes years of healing before the natural trust is restored, and it is likely never to heal unless an event takes place in the life of that person that causes a 'conversion,' a renewal of faith in human nature. The greatest gift parents can give their children is basic trust, and when they fail, the children are damaged, possibly for life.

But when things have gone well in childhood and the growing person is able to enter a trusting relationship, much depends on his or her good fortune (or destiny) to meet the person who can reciprocate that trust. There are many lonely people who long for a trusting relationship but cannot find the one who would respond at that level. When they explore a friendship they come up against a flaw and so find that they cannot confide. It is a delicate matter. A confiding relationship can be helped to come about by asking a person for help or advice. This generally calls forth a positive response, provided the favour doesn't ask too much. By enabling the other person to give, you open the way to communication, and you can then explain how your need came about. In doing this you have been open about your being unable to manage the problem on your own; your thankfulness at the end of the encounter will promote the warmth in the soul of that person.

Such an encounter can form the ground of a relationship, and from then on it is a matter of seeing if it will deepen. Whilst relationships appear to have their own dynamic, they do respond to being worked on. Indeed we have to take responsibility for the growth of our relationships and for keeping the contact alive and active. This will be required of us more and more as time passes in the present phase of our evolution: we are in the age of individualism, so we have to build our confiding relationships on the basis of the yearning of people to be seen and respected as individuals, rather than as members of a particular group.

Confidence in a relationship encourages a two-way sharing. Indeed, that is vital: otherwise the one who only listens and does not share will appear like a counsellor or interrogator, and the relationship cannot flourish. But when it is two-way, open and affords a good basis for exchange, both participants will find that they will delve more deeply into themselves and begin to reveal their more hidden feelings. This helps both to be congruent, that is, to speak out exactly what they feel without the need to hold back or cover up.

Conversations that are open in this way can release a great deal of tension, shame and frustration.

Moreover they can lead through intimacy to self-knowledge: 'I get to know myself by letting you know me.' And self-knowledge is the way to wisdom.

Intimacy can be of spirit, or of soul, or of body. Those who are spiritually intimate can share what is most inward of ideals, spiritual experiences and the longing to transcend the earthly sense-world. Usually the path of spiritual development is a lonely one, but it is a wonderful grace to have a companion on the path. This overcomes a deep loneliness that could otherwise be felt.

Intimacy of the soul is what works between good

friends, who know each other's aims and fears, strengths and weaknesses. The teenage girl and her girl friend open their hearts to each other; a man who carries a big load of responsibility needs someone with whom he can confide his worries and admit his own inadequacy before taking a vital decision; and a woman needs a woman friend who will listen to her difficulties and disappointments, as well as her hopes and expectations. But such friends must be able to keep all these matters confidential: there must occur no leaks. For it is devastating if someone confides in another and then hears it from a third person.

Intimacy of body is a mystery. Our physical body carries us through life; it supports our endeavours and bears our sorrows and setbacks. It is an organism of consummate wisdom, and of magical complexity. Just to think of the amazing structure and working of the eye, or the ear, or of the organ of balance: we can be full of wonder that such a marvel is possible, and it is you and I. Yet intimacy in the sphere of the body invades holy ground. Exposure of the body can destroy the dignity of a person when it is aggressively demanded. There is a deep reluctance to being seen naked, stemming allegorically from the event in Paradise when Adam and Eve bit into the apple of the Tree of Knowledge, and were suddenly ashamed of their nakedness before God. And yet intimacy of body belongs to the rituals of love-making. But the conditions must be right. The onrush of shame can make the idyllic feel sordid if the intimacy ceases to be upheld by a high degree of mutual confidence.

Intimacy at any of the three levels needs agreement between those who enter its hallowed portals. The agreement entails respect, tact, gentleness and awareness of each other. The breaking of the agreement shatters the intimacy, and sympathy turns instantly into antipathy. Many breakdowns in committed relationships can be traced back to a moment when the sweetness of intimacy turned sour. It is helpful to make the agreement a conscious one, entered into freely by both partners. For intimacy heals the plight of loneliness. And yet it resembles solitude: it is a sharing of that which belongs to oneself in one's quiet and most inward moments. In intimacy barriers are dropped, boundaries dissolve: there is openness and communing. Feeling can flow and love weaves its bond. In a woman her mother-instinct is stirred, caring, nurturing, holding and keeping the experiences in her heart. Whereas a man meets his lesser-known self and finds a well springing up, full of a gentle reassurance of his own worth and the worth of his friend.

Intimacy calls for confidence, in all its meanings. The confiding relationship is a source of growth-in-security and mutual regard. It overcomes bitterness, anger, fear and shame. In its truth it makes one free. It shows what can be the grace of marriage.

# 18. Sexuality:
# a very personal matter

It is striking to notice how openly we speak about sexuality in general, and the sexual behaviour of others, but treat our own sexual actions as personal and private. Our present Western culture has no qualms about discussing and publicizing the behaviour of prominent people, but we would all find it totally unfair if our own behaviour were to be made into a talking-point or common knowledge, even if we have nothing to be ashamed of.

Our own sexuality and indeed our own sex organs are not for all to see and know. This reticence overtook Adam and Eve when they suddenly could see their physical bodies, when they 'fell' because of Lucifer's enticement with the apple from the Tree of Knowledge. They had fallen out of innocence, out of nature, out of Paradise: they could see each other as physical and not spiritual. So they covered their genitals with fig-leaves. The wild fig was used in ancient rituals to enhance the power of reproduction and fertility. So we can surmise that the fig-leaf was not used to cover up nakedness but as a sign that human beings, from Adam and Eve onwards, were endowed with the power to regenerate physically, and this was not dependent on the working of divine spirit.[12]

Why this reticence? Perhaps really because one's own sexuality cannot be shared unless there is a situation of trust with another person, a very particular quality of trust. 'Through my sexuality I give myself away!' This is a strange phenomenon, because what we wish to keep secret is scarcely startling or exceptional or unknown.

This feeling of reticence is perhaps unconsciously based on a sense of awe and wonder at the power with which we are entrusted when we reach puberty. The power to bring about the life of another human being; the power of creating Man. Originally this divine power was guided by the gods; then for a time it was entrusted to priests, then to leaders of peoples, and then further downwards to families and clans. In the process the exercise of this power has been more and more freed from restrictions and taboos, from the racial, religious and tribal customs: until in our time, in most cultures of the world, the right to procreate has come into the hands of all individuals, without even the moral requirement of marriage and commitment. Sex has become a personal matter, and the widespread attitude in Western cultures is that no-one has the right to tell another what he or she is allowed to do.

All this has its good side. In our time already the individual person can aspire to moral freedom: there is in each person a core of morality. There is no need to be stultified by a society of double standards or a 'culture' of negative pressures. Responsibility for sexual behaviour has devolved onto each person: and the individual has to work out a personal ethic in accordance with what is meaningful. Restrictions and enticements coming from outside of oneself can be neutralized by a strong inner standpoint. Our time heralds a far-reaching transformation; we need to recognize it. Mankind *can* now rise to a fuller stature. Our spiritual component is no longer remote from us; it is 'at hand.' It is now on us to take ourselves seriously as the source and guardian of our own morality.

This picture may seem unduly hopeful. We are creatures of habit, instinctual drives and selfish appetites; we are driven largely by our emotions, and these are only rarely pervaded by sweetness and light. There is also the retarding effect of shame and the vengeful force of jealousy: we have to succeed, and we fight to win. The complex mixture that is found in male and female persons causes the human being to be vulnerable to the negative enticement of pride and the drive of power. All this has to be reckoned with. And our own sexuality is endowed with a seemingly inexhaustible power which is both arrogant and seductive, and gives rise to confusion as well as aggression. So are not such expectations somewhat naive?

Instincts have long had the upper hand. We have become familiar with aggressive and wanton behaviour, with the present-day prevalence of abuse and harassment, with the practice of turning women into sex symbols. We scarcely realize that the crossing of the boundary of another person's integrity is violation. But this time should now change; it belongs to the past. The self that is spiritual is required to assert its leadership. This is not a sacrificing of freedom but a fulfilment of it: in becoming consciously responsible for our own actions, we ourselves become congruent. And the world around us will reap the benefit.

A deep-going philosophy of life, a *Weltanschauung*, needs to be encouraged, in such a way that the intellectual growth of persons is balanced by a development of social responsibility. Dogmas, precepts, moral imperatives and imposed standards will not succeed. Today's young persons have to work at their own grasp of the meaning of life, and to allow their own wellspring of goodness to shape their personal behaviour. Teenagers experience sexuality as an issue for which there is little guidance: maybe they seldom ask for it, perhaps sensing that few adults are clear enough to give it. Instead they model themselves on the mature person who has lively values and a cheerful self-discipline: one who is contented, in touch and in harmony.

Mankind has entered a new stage of development. The guiding hand of society and religion, working on the person from outside, can now be replaced by an inner disposition to act responsibly: a disposition to act out of oneself without outer coercion, schooling oneself and guiding one's life in a way that harmonizes our own interests with the interests of fellow human beings. This should even extend to concern for the preservation of the environment and the conserving of valuable cultural achievements. Society still needs to present boundaries and to impose penalties for transgressing them, but these will become less and less relevant. Modern persons, with their own inner freedom, will be able to transcend outer dictates and act out of the spiritual values of their true selves. This is the new 'bonding-again' with the spirit, which can be called, in the true sense of the word, the renewal of religion.

There is a growing conviction that inter-personal actions need to respect boundaries: we need to overcome the temptation to invade another's privacy without consent. Within this climate there will come about a recognition of the spiritual and psychological effects of sexual activity: the change will begin within the individual, through a raising of awareness. The man will become more aware of what sex means to a woman, and not only be spurred on by his own self-indulgent desires. And the woman will develop sympathy for the vulnerability that so often threatens a man's time-honoured image.

Gradually too a deeper awareness of the working of sexual intercourse will grow: for instance that every act involves life forces and spiritual energies which, if thwarted by contraception, create turmoil in the spiritual auras of those involved.

Moreover the effects of abortions will become more known, and abortion will be increasingly unacceptable to those who contemplate it, even if the state and society condone it. The suffering of the foetus will no longer be ignored. These rejected souls enter the aura of the earth, and it will require immense atonement to release them into the realms of the spiritual world. Mother Teresa has many times warned that we cannot expect peace on earth between factions and nations while the practice of abortion is condoned. Awareness of this is set to grow.

Altogether a new moral consciousness towards sexual activity will arise within thinking human beings. This will happen even without the fear and dire warning that comes with the phenomenon of AIDS, although the full impact of the pandemic is yet to be experienced. Such progress in spiritual awareness cannot come about as the product of fear and loss. If it is to be effective in transforming our attitudes towards sex, it will have to grow out of positive forces within the human psyche: not out of a negative response to the fear of death, but out of forces of love, reverence and conscience.

This coming state of soul may still be far off for humanity as a whole, but scattered islands of healthy living can anticipate the future and lead the way towards it.

o O o

Such a view is based on the conviction that the human person is progressing in consciousness. Formerly somewhat dreamy in his awareness of the physical world, man has evolved to become fully and clearly conscious of his material environment: but this has meant forfeiting the awareness and conscious experience of the spiritual aspects of his own being and his surroundings. We believe we see clearly when we look at a flower or a bush: but in fact our ordinary eyes do not see the formative forces that surround that flower or bush, the life-giving aura that gives form and sustenance to the plant. This is only visible to the eye of an initiate.

However, the way towards a renewed spiritual perception has begun in present-day human evolving; this is not to be a reversion to a state of natural clairvoyance, but a going forward with individual freedom to gain a higher vision. The emphasis is on inner freedom, and on one's own activity.

The faculty for perceiving the hidden worlds of spirit-forces can only be acquired through steady and selfless application. The appropriate disposition of soul will be a matter of evolution, but the actual attainment of such vision will require conscientious dedication to the necessary exercises and disciplines, coupled with a strong development of morality through reverence and clarity of observation. The way forward is already available for those who want to embark on this quest. Attainment of such vision would replace our instinctual sexual drive with awareness of the true meaning of sexuality, as well as of its dangers.

However, we are only at the foothills of this ascent. As yet sexual aberrations are widespread: from sexual abuse of children, rape, prostitution, to pornography and various degrees of harassment. The prevalence of such abuse is evidence of a lack of self-control and considerateness, and indeed of understanding of human interaction on a sexual basis. All this is a strong reminder that sex is mysterious and its abuse is enticing.

Sex always has to do with beginnings, with birth. Just as violence has to do with endings, with death. Sex touches on the new; it can bring about a new state in relationship, renewing and revitalizing. A deep truth underlies all earthly existence: everything in life is a trinity. So too with man and woman. I alone am incomplete; I search for a means of moving from singleness to duality by finding my partner: but this is ultimately not satisfying or stable in itself; only if we together achieve the third is there fulfilment. The third is not only the product of the two; it has its own entity and being: thereby it can complete the process. The duality belongs to the present; the third bears the future within it.

In the past the third was the child born of the sexual relating of the two. Nowadays this is often not the aim nor the result. Thereby if sexual action remains dual and does not reach the triad, it is not fulfilling except for a momentary expansion of consciousness with its attendant elation. It remains in the realm of beginnings rather than completion: an appetizer and not a meal.

If sexual activity does not have procreation as its aim, how can it achieve the third element? What makes it fulfilling? Two people love each other: and they have the longing to know each other better in order to explore their connection. There is the urge to be close in the deepest possible way, which means going fully into a sexual relationship: this asks for intimacy and mutual giving; it allows energies to flow, emotional release and a great feeling of relaxation. There seems to be no necessity for this to be encapsulated in marriage: it is a spontaneous expression of vibrant love.

Such couples enter into sexual activity with great hopes for delight, release and mutual confirmation; there is the expectation of gaining new energy, of empowerment and a deepening of love for each other. Yet often the outcome is exhaustion, loneliness, shattering of self-esteem, fear of consequences, and a withering of the relationship. The arrow has missed its target; in place of enhanced harmony, there is anger of a subtle kind; in place of warmth and mutuality, a wish to dissolve the scene and leave no traces. In place of fun, a feeling of sleaze.

What goes wrong? Sex outside of marriage used to be considered a sin; indeed it is still condemned by most religions. Adultery is a heavy word. And yet the mores of our time accept sexual activity and living together irrespective of marriage as part of the process that may lead to marriage or may not. Marriage is seen as a dispensable restriction, and divorce as part of the scenario of the marriage-contract.

Every young person meets the question: should I not explore this aspect of life? Chastity, in the sense of complete abstaining from sexual activity, has little appeal. There is hardly any reticence in seeking the experience. A recent careful survey carried out in America found that, irrespective of the racial and ethnic groups to which they belong, almost half the teenagers are already having sexual relations with a partner, and 80% have had sexual experience by the time they are twenty.[13] This may sound very permissive, but a new trend is also appearing: teenager sex seems to be declining in regularity. This may have to do with the fear of AIDS, but it may be a sign that sex is ceasing to be the 'big deal' for adolescents.

 o O o

This is a very private matter. Yet it involves at least two persons, possibly also a child that is born, and at times other persons as well. It is said that when two people are in love with each other, it is their freedom to express this love in their own way. Still more extreme is the point of view that whatever you can get away with is allowed. Yet the condemnation of pre-marital sex by many religions is categorical, although their apologists are seldom able to give reasons: they rely on quotations from their scriptures.

Maybe a new understanding of chastity is relevant in our time. Total abstinence from sexual activity would not be expected: but it should not be entered into without due reverence for the partner and for the deed. Experimentation for its own sake, and wanton involvement with sex, would be out. But a genuine and mutual wish for closeness, in loyalty and affection, would uphold this new approach to chastity.

The study mentioned above points to an interesting difference in the motivation of men and women experiencing sexual relations for the first time. With men, 90% wanted it; less than 8% 'went along with it.' About half were impelled by curiosity, a quarter by affection; few could say they were in love with their first partner. With women 70% wanted it, 24% 'went along,' 4% were forced. Only a quarter were motivated by curiosity, while half experienced real affection for their partner. One laconic remark tells much: 'Virtually no women said that they wanted or went along with sex for physical pleasure.'[14]

It is pertinent to consider the spiritual aspects. The sexual energies are biological, driven by emotions, yet they serve the highest power that is entrusted to humans: that of creating life. It is a divine power, given to us to use in harmony with the aims of human destiny. Sexual activity enables souls to incarnate; when one goes through the motions but frustrates the fulfilment, there is the danger of dragging down the holiest faculty to the level of the instinctual and emotional, a far cry from the noble nature of the deed. Hence the strange feeling of unworthiness that can set in directly afterwards, a feeling of uncleanness, embarrassment, a strange longing 'to be elsewhere.'

Conscience has its say: 'You have entered the holiest area of human existence without reverence.' What had been a growing relationship of love can be abruptly stopped: sex proves to be very different from love.

Here lies the crucial fact: love and sex cannot be equated. They are opposites in regard to selflessness. Love is selfless. Sexual energy is self-relating; the aim is a special experience for oneself.

A guideline for appropriate behaviour could be 'Whatever makes you feel good afterwards.' Or 'Whatever enables love to grow in unselfishness and the power to give.'

Yet, as we have seen, sex can be more than 'sex,' and the selfish aspect can be transformed through the power of love. Moreover, whilst the male activity can be even brutally selfish, the female part is, by nature, giving. Yet a woman's acceptance of pre-marital sex is generally spurred on by a mixture of motives, each with a self-regarding component. She may fear that a refusal would kill the relationship; she may have the hope that by saying 'yes' she will lead the man to marriage. Another consequence can be that the woman becomes more possessive and the man less interested. When this happens the romantic bubble bursts.

Pre-marital sex often occurs in moments of reduced consciousness; for instance under the influence of alcohol. The sobering up process afterwards can be ghastly, especially if the two have really no commitment to the relationship. From the outset pre-marital sex acquires its own dynamic. Yet it contains a built-in stress: the commitment is unclear. Is the aim the growth of a bond of love between the partners? Or to get to know each other better? Or perhaps to oblige the reluctant partner to make a commitment? Or to break down barriers of reticence and restraint? In the beginning any of these could be the case;

but as soon as the sex becomes sex-for-its-own-sake, all such aims are forgotten.

What is a man's attitude to a woman who is known to sleep around? Would he reject her as a potential marriage partner, even if he himself has a similar past? Attitudes are becoming more open and accepting. A woman who feels herself to be unloved, insecure, inadequate, may grasp at the chance for a sex-encounter to give her a better self-image as a potential marriage-partner. If a woman is in love she could be more open to pre-marital sex; if the man is in love his inclinations in this regard may diminish.

The art of loving, like any art, takes work and training in order to develop. What used to be the time of courtship and engagement is nowadays seldom formalized. The old sequence of courtship, marriage and the starting of the family is often reversed: first comes the child; then, perhaps, the marriage; and only thereafter the working at mutual adjustment and the getting to know each other. When the baby comes as a result of pre-marital sex, the relationship between the parents has a difficult start. It may break down altogether, with the mother remaining single; but even if they marry the relationship may well be burdened by anger, unless this is carefully worked through with counselling and openness.

The anger, mixed with blame, is due to the feeling 'You got me into this!' on the part of the mother and often of the father. Both are suddenly obliged to adjust their life-styles, perhaps alter their career plans and, in the case of the woman, undertake premature motherhood. If the couple do not marry she will have an especially hard task. She has to try to be both mother and father, and she knows that her child will always be at a disadvantage through lack of an effective father. Her career plan or study programme is likely to be brought to a standstill for some years at least, and so she has to cope with financial hardship as well as aloneness and possibly a lack of emotional support. Often the presence of a child reduces her chance of finding a marriage partner.

The unfolding of awareness and responsibility outlined earlier in this chapter is happening. The survey quoted above shows that young people today give much more thought to these matters than they are credited for: those who uphold a wait-and-grow policy and manage to sustain it are the silent majority. Love is only possible in freedom, and sex is fulfilling only if based on freedom and not on unconscious drives. True freedom is a benefit that comes from commitment: we are only truly free when the basis of our life is secure. But we live in an age of freedom, and so our decisions on moral behaviour must be our own, original and convincing for ourselves. There has to be a deeper motivation for avoiding pre-marital sex than respect for ancient taboos and long-standing prohibitions. This motivation must arise out of our own consciousness.

We seldom discuss the promptings of our sexuality with anyone, least of all the present partner. It is hardly romantic to lay out our yearnings on the dissecting table, to explore their components and the 'compelling dynamic' that unites them into a boisterous urge. So it is important to do our own thinking beforehand. Thinking that can pierce through the emotions, and light up the eternal Self that nourishes our ideals, our values and our understanding of life.

Sexuality engages the forces of life: and we need to face the question 'Are they ours to use as we wish?' Against this background we will be able to explore the phenomena of love, togetherness, mutual regard and other aspects of relating, as surveyed in the earlier chapters of this book.

All this will prepare us for the vital questions of our actual building of relationship. Do we really want the intimacy of sex? Is our friendship strong enough to bear the crossing of a Rubicon that 'consummation' involves? How will it be afterwards: joy or regrets? What kind of a commitment to each other do we have? What actually are our motives?

Such questions lead us to the mystery of sex as such, pointing to the differences between man and woman in soul and feeling. But they also lead inescapably into our own situation.

It may seem ridiculous to think this way. Must we again face that awful dogma that love and sex have little to do with each other and certainly cannot be identified? Where is the joy, the fun, in all this questioning? We are entering the twenty-first century, the new millennium. We know our freedom and our rights, and we know what we are doing!

This chapter is not *against* anything but *for* the truth: only the truth can give us the freedom we are seeking. We are concerned with a deepening of relationship and commitment: if this comes about, the purely sexual aspect will be only a component of a wider dynamic that will foster the love that bonds the couple. This can lead to bonding and not bondage: there can then be romantic love, full of health and its own wisdom, and indeed of goodness, in the process and in its fulfilment. All this will bring us to the heart of the matter, deepening our knowledge of the human being.

Is there any other experience that compares with orgasm? Maybe religious ecstasy is in some ways similar, but indeed orgasm is unique in human experience, in its intensity and dynamism. We can question, evaluate and form an appraisal of whatever leads up to it and the circumstances in which it occurs: but the actual experience is 'out of this world.' As momentary as it is, it touches on the eternal: it is concentrated now-ness, transcending before and after. It makes available to our experience the quality of the eternal-now. For an instant body, soul and spirit merge, in unity with the wholeness of our partner. Spontaneous receiving and giving are celebrated, engendering an explosion of new feeling.

Ideally. But were we adequately prepared to go through this together? Did we realize what heights and depths would open to us? Can we come back to our everyday separate existence and just go on? How can we even share what we went through together, when we have no words, no language or concepts that can do justice to the space we entered? Or was all this marred for you by the way I acted? Or should I reveal that I suffered agony because it was not truly shared by you? Do we not need to work at our friendship, before we are ready to be soul-body-and-spiritual mates? Without this can there be any real carrying-strength in our togetherness? Or any true intimacy? Does all this tell us that our love has not yet ripened?

The enjoyment of sex requires greatness of heart; it appears to be so natural and easy, so uncomplicated, but it is far more than all these. It is always physical, emotional and spiritual, and so engages all three of these aspects of our being; if we are conscious of only one, or two, of these aspects, there is lack of fulfilment. Like any realm of experience it has its demands, and we are rewarded when we meet them but suffer the consequences of failure. It asks for awareness, integrity and a sense for discovery.

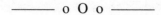

Sexual activity is as important as it is free. This view has become fairly general, since the nineteen-sixties inaugurated the sexual revolution in western society. Film-goers and magazine-readers absorb erotic scenes and stories that persuade them that they are missing out on what 'most' people are 'enjoying.' Sex is supposedly available without restriction, equally safe from unwanted pregnancy and from the risk of AIDS. And society doesn't mind: no-one who is lively, healthy and vibrant is holding back.

Earlier in-depth surveys have promoted or supported this idea, but their methods of sampling and analysis have proved to be misleading. Yet the recent study has shown that the actual situation is by no means free. Society as a whole (if we think of the total inhabitants of a country) can exert little influence on general behaviour: but sub-groups within society exert a powerful influence in all directions, and likewise on the sexual activities of their adherents. These sub-groups are unclearly defined though basically homogeneous groups of people sharing similar characteristics: yet they have a decisive influence on the behaviour of those who belong to them. Indeed, whilst this is an age in which persons strive to become truly individual, this process is far from complete. There is a longing among many people to achieve autonomy, to become fully authentic persons; but meanwhile the sub-group to which they each belong exerts a surprisingly strong restrictive power.

We tend to associate with people like ourselves, with whom we have a good deal in common. People who share our language and general culture, our educational achievement and religious background. We choose people of our own age, who share our ideals, our economic status and our system of values. Among 'our people' we find our friends: and it is with them that sexual relationships are most likely to develop. Those who experiment with casual relationships outside of their own circle, or move away from their own kind, are a relatively small proportion.

In short, affinity of background counts in relationship: race, ethnicity, education, religion, age. Something more than sexual attraction is needed to develop a partnership. Quite naturally we wish for someone who has a similar way of life, and therefore the circle of people from whom we can select a partner is fairly restricted. Such affinity is even helpful in short-term relationships, whilst marriages having this advantage are known to last longer and be less prone to stress. The survey (mainly covering the United States, but also U.K., France and Finland) shows that an overwhelming majority of both women and men have only one sexual partner for long periods of time. The modern idea that 'I cannot know you deeply unless I know you sexually' does not really apply. Rather the question is 'How can I dare to know you sexually before I know who you are and what we have in common?'

So there is a paradox. We pride ourselves on our rugged individualism and our ample choice in sexual partnering: yet our search is shaped by the pattern of our lives so far; we tend to fix onto what we are used to. We like those whom we are like; we are influenced by what others think about what we are doing. We are social beings, belonging to our group and adhering to its subtle rules, and this affects much of our behaviour, including the finding of our partners. Its guidelines even tell us how often we should have sex and what we should do, what risks to recognize regarding AIDS, and what to expect from our partner in terms of a commitment.

The result of this is that there is much less sexual activity than is popularly believed. And the choice of sexual partners is very much more restricted than is usually imagined. There are many people who, in fact, have it very difficult to find a satisfying relationship that involves full sexual expression. The more individual we become, the stronger our wish to find a partner who shares our interests: we are more and more dependent on finding a partner who will agree. 'Where shall we go to eat? What music shall we listen to?' The more we aspire to be ourselves, the more vital it becomes that our friend will not undermine our self-ness by demanding quite other kinds of environment or adherence to other customs. Compatibility becomes an increasingly sensitive issue as our frail ego makes its way towards independence and self-expression. Our individualness needs such support until it becomes established spiritually and humanly, and this prompts us to seek constant approval from our network of friends, as well as from our partner.

When human beings are able to know themselves truly and spiritually, it will become easier to form friendships with others very different from ourselves. But that time lies far ahead. By then a new social order will have been achieved; mankind will have become a brotherhood of morally activated persons. Until this development is attained, we need ongoing confirmation of our individual worth from those with whom we naturally associate.

This new time will bring a change in our instincts. As we develop in all-round spiritual humanness, the sexual side of our nature will subside as the driving-force: the power of feeling will replace the raw energy of our emotions, and sexuality will lose its present importance. In the still-further future the whole procedure for procreation will change; it will involve the larynx and the creative power of the word. All this lies beyond the scope of our present study: we are only concerned with companionship today. But when we act out of our true selves, we can know that we are at the same time helping to achieve the next goals in human evolution.

The survey we are quoting gives interesting general background. Although most people find their partners within their own sub-group or network, the criteria for finding a suitable partner are similar in all groups, regardless of their differences: patterns repeat themselves, whether it is the affluent WASP, the upward-mobile black, the Christian Right, and so on, in America, or the various groups in other countries.

The romantic ideals of intelligence, charm, gentleness, beauty and affluence don't usually come together in a single package; real life seldom brings love at first sight with an alluring stranger that turns into a long-term happy marriage, and most shipboard romances go adrift after a while. Finding a partner is like entering a market in which one is a buyer and a seller: there is limited choice. I must find the one whom I like and who likes me: and we must be like each other in our general approach to life. Partnership is an ongoing all-round sharing; marriage is a committed sharing of everything. Most couples meet in quite conventional ways, within their network; and if the network fails to produce a partner, the way ahead may remain lonely. There is no magic formula. But there is destiny, and the network we belong to is part of our destiny.

———— o O o ————

The survey also reveals other trends. The number of men and women who are virgins at marriage is gradually rising: forty years ago the proportion was high; it then dipped drastically, and now seems to be moving upwards again. However, living together of unmarried couples was rare forty years ago, whereas now it is common. The survey states:

> Like other recent studies, ours shows a marked shift toward living together rather than marriage as the first union of couples. With an increase in cohabitation, the distinctions among having a steady sexual partner, a live-in sexual partner, and a marriage have gotten more fuzzy. This shift began at the same time as talk of a sexual revolution. Our study shows that people who came of age before 1970 almost invariably got married without first living together, while the younger people seldom did. But, we find, the average age at which people first move in with a partner — either by marrying, or living together — has remained nearly constant, around age twenty-two for men and twenty for women. The difference is now that the first union is increasingly likely to be a cohabitation.[15]

By the age of thirty, three quarters of all Americans are either married or living with someone, which means they have partnered and not casual sex. Yet the regularity of sex declines after this age.

A different factor also contributes to this decline is the number of women who at mid-life are driven out of partnerships through a breakdown in relationship with their men. Men in this situation seem to find new partners, whilst women are at a great disadvantage and only seldom establish a new partnership. For these women it is not a matter of losing interest or a change in hormones: it is a decline in opportunity. They will be reluctant to engage in occasional sex without a basis of affection or commitment.

—— o O o ——

A contented sexual life and a happy life in general go together. Some may be convinced that the quality of sex life is the foundation of happiness, but most would agree that it is the other way round. Sexuality plays its part, but the total human person derives meaning and satisfaction from the achievement of Selfhood rather than indulgence in the driving force of libido. For both man and woman the attainment of spiritual aspirations provides a basis for a meaningful life, one which can cope with daily problems and meet the crisis-points of destiny. Such a life can also enable the partners to see the good in all people and all of nature, and enjoy the inflowing of new ideas. We are called upon to become masters: free, authentic, buoyant; able to face challenges with courage and a deep trust in our own potential. And our own sexuality is one of those challenges: it can contribute to our wellbeing or cause turmoil, depending on how we master it.

# 19. Creation or recreation?

Sexuality certainly raises many issues. What does it serve? Clearly it is for creating new life. A woman and a man join their forces in order to bring about a child. This child remains their joint responsibility until it attains adulthood, and thereafter the family bonding remains significant. We have all derived our life from the sexual deed of our parents. It is thanks to sex that there are people on the earth.

But sexuality has another aspect: the act of sexual togetherness is able to rejuvenate, refresh and deepen a relationship, and kindle new energies in a woman and a man: it can be a deed of love, an expression of openness and a confirming of commitment. There is enjoyment and release of tension; it can transform anger and fear into harmony. And it can open the souls towards higher spiritual ideals and insights. Yet all this that is positive and beneficial can be turned into something negative, unpleasant and destructive, if certain conditions are not adhered to. There has to be mutual openness and warmth, sensitivity for how the other is feeling, an awareness of the forces that are engaged; there needs to be agreement. The more this agreement is verbalized and the less it is assumed, the less is the likelihood of disappointment and hurt. This may sound unromantic and a denial of spontaneity, but we don't live in a male-dominated world any more, nor is it appropriate to use sexuality to relieve basic instincts. In our age of individual consciousness, such behaviour is retrograde.

So creation and recreation: are these two sides of the

same thing? They are two sides of sexuality, but how do they go together? The answer is that they have indeed gone apart. Because of the widespread use of contraception, the recreational side of sexuality has largely been separated from the creative aspect of conceiving. The appearance of the Pill has freed women from the fear of pregnancy. And the consequences of falling pregnant when unmarried have eased in terms of the attitude of society. A considerable proportion of people no longer regard sexual intercourse outside of marriage as unusual or sinful. Two generations ago a child born out of 'wedlock' carried the stigma of illegitimacy and suffered ostracism. Now this is accepted in many cultures and the word is no longer used: the bastard has become the love child. African societies have always regarded the conceiving of children as a blessing, an enrichment and something natural. In the Western world nowadays such children are able to accept this status without awareness of any stigma.

Yet all this is not without problems: in urbanized African communities the extended families are strained in their economic resources, whilst the inflated birth-rate leads to a vast amount of unemployment and poverty, with the resultant crime and violence. In western communities there is a measure of state welfare to relieve the economic burden, but the fatherless child is missing something that the state can't provide.

The more open attitude to sex is a significant phenomenon and belongs to the challenges of our time. In ages past the expression of sexuality used to be guided by the priests: it entailed sacred rituals, such that spirituality and sexuality were not seen as opposites but as belonging together. Gradually the expression of sexuality has become more and more emancipated from restrictions and taboos, and even from social mores, until in our time individuals are virtually free to engage in sexual activity according to the promptings of personal desire. As it is such a widespread phenomenon nowadays, it is better to recognize it than merely to condemn it on the basis of what was acceptable in the past. Sexuality for creation and sexuality as recreation both have a place in the ordinary life of a large proportion of men and women.

Are we to aspire to a re-uniting of these two aspects? Are we to understand and uphold what still remains a moral prescription of various religious groups? The Catholic Church condemns any non-natural intervention to prevent conception, and regards sex outside of marriage as sinful. Such teachings, based on deep truth, have guided humanity through the centuries: they were needed then. This would mean using sex always in the creative mode, unless conception is avoided by restricting the event to the days in the woman's cycle when conception would not take place. However, western man in general is far from adopting this approach. Modern individualism rejects prescription and proscription. Today the individual takes personal responsibility: it is up to each person to work out what is right, clearly and intuitively, and then have the strength of character to uphold it.

There is no point in arguing the rights and wrongs of contraception. But we can move forward from where we are today, towards a new ethic for all sexual activity, in particular recreational sex. First we can call to mind how things can go wrong:

— There could be an absence of mutuality because of the dominance of one partner.
— Through a lack of gentleness: for instance the man needs to realize how tender and easily hurt the woman is physically in the sexual area, and so wait

till the woman is ready. Or else the woman can hurt the man's pride if she ridicules his performance when it flounders.

— The man can withdraw after his climax instead of being with the woman emotionally just when she is most open and vulnerable.

— The woman can be so uptight that she does not really give herself.

— He can make her feel like a prostitute by the way he concentrates only on the physical experience.

— She can be simply bored by the encounter and wish it to be over and finished with.

A sexual meeting could be treated as a holy event, full of reverence for the partner and also for the event itself. For holy substances and vessels are used, and life forces are engaged. These forces can be enhanced and enriched by the power of love, or they can be desecrated. The deep and sensitive feelings of each partner can be honoured with gentleness or violated in brashness.

To help to ensure that the experience is a good one, preparation is vital. The day is special; the participants clear away any distractions and relax tensions. Souls strive for peacefulness and the resolving of any conflicts. Thoughts take on sublime contents; a feeling for beauty is called up through a listening conversation and a sharing of the poetry of the inward heart. 'We shall be meeting deeply, giving and receiving.' The time has to be generous, the space comfortable and safe; privacy assured. Two souls in harmony, two spiritual persons in communion with each other, two bodies ready to celebrate intimacy in selfless giving. The full meaning of re-creation can be realized, and sexuality can take on a quality that totally frees it from all sordidness.

There would be rejoicing in heaven if the incredible privilege and power which has been handed over to human beings could be turned into an offering and not be used for mere self-indulgence. Then maybe the creative aspect of sexuality would find a connection again to the recreational, and the dichotomy between sacred and profane would fall away. Sex as such would be re-admitted to the temple of Humanity and no longer be banished from within its hallowed walls.

Another way of putting this is to recall our consideration of love, and see that sexuality is raised from the level of *hubris,* through *eros,* to arrive at *philia* and aspire to *agapé.* Then we will rightly use the term 'to make love.'

How much would change if there could be such considerateness for the well-being of one's sexual partner! Such consciousness, radiating through the psyche of individual men and women, could have an effect on modern culture. And maybe put an end to the scourge of AIDS.

# 20. The question of marriage

Marriage is in question. Is it still the rock that stands firm in the eddying stream of society? Or has it been swept away in the torrent of change which society is experiencing?

Marriages do indeed take place, but nearly half of them crumble and disappear. Is marriage still part of our natural landscape?

So, even when marriages have been entered into, they are proving far from permanent. Difficulties between marriage partners are no longer accepted as grist to the mill that refines their relationship. Nowadays they are seen as a good reason to go apart and lay aside the commitment.

Today there is no need to marry in order to satisfy the expectations of society. (This is as much a comment on the state of society as it is on the state of marriage.) Children can be born irrespective of their parents being married: the stigma of illegitimacy has largely dissolved.

The roles of men and women, once so clear, are now blurred: he as breadwinner, she as home-maker. Most women also work: the family economy requires this. Women have shaken off the shackles of dependency, and no longer require marriage for their status.

So what purpose does marriage serve? Ideally, three purposes.

Firstly, it solemnizes the commitment of the marriage partners to each other; it is a declaring of their intent to stand by each other through the rest of life, and it asks for the recognition and support of all who wish to see it prosper.

Secondly, marriage is a legal contract, regularizing the relationship between husband and wife as part of the structure of society. It clarifies issues in advance in respect of division of assets in the event of a breakdown in the marriage, and it gives the courts the power to make settlements regarding the care of children should the marriage end in divorce. So there is a comprehensive legal involvement entailed in marriage.

And thirdly, marriage is still frequently confirmed in a religious ceremony which blesses the couple in their decision to build a communal life together.

The first of these aspects of marriage is a matter primarily between the two spouses. The second is a sign that marriage still has a place in the social organization of the state in which the couple contract their marriage. The third goes beyond the couple and society and involves the unseen world of the spirit. The first two aspects of marriage commend themselves respectively to a well-ordered relationship and a well-structured society. Yet the first no longer needs to be formalized and, as regards the second, society is accepting couples who live together but do not enter into a legal arrangement.

The main question around marriage concerns the third aspect, the religious and spiritual. Sometimes a religious marriage is sought for because it is morally binding; sometimes it is avoided just because it is morally binding. Has the divine world any part to play in what two people on earth intend to do together? Are not human beings in our time emancipated from the requirement to refer all that they do to God? And anyway, if God is the creative essence of the entire universe, what possible interest could such a great being have in how we conduct our lives as tiny dots on the

earth, the earth itself being a tiny speck in the whole universe? Or else, if God is like Big Brother monitoring our
every movement, why should we pay court to such an inter-
fering, inquisitive and judgmental know-all?

But then, what is man? It is helpful to be reminded how
much we depend on the beings in the spiritual world for our
continuing existence on earth. Our soul-life is sustained
through the inspiration of thoughts and ideas. Our state of
openness depends on the way feeling is flowing through it,
and with it our power to love. Our will-impulses are far from
mechanical; they embody a sense for morality. And our
morality is guided by a sense for what is right. We act
morally when we act in accordance with one or both of these
testing questions: Is this the kind of action we would expect
to see happening in heaven? or Would I do this if God were
here with me and would see my actions? If this kind of
awareness remains alive in a person, he develops a sense for
the nearness of the spirit and its relevance in the daily life. We
come from heaven, and after our time on earth we are called
back to heaven. A major component of our humanity is lost
if we deny the spiritual element in our lives: it is like trying
to breathe in a stuffy atmosphere. And we live in constant
fear of what will happen to us when we die.

Yet we do not 'report back' to the spirit only when we die.
We do so every night when we sleep: for then our Self is free
to commune with our guardian angel and work through the
experiences of the day, with its good and bad deeds and its
unfinished agenda. Our Self is in touch with the spiritual
world in a real way, even though all consciousness of the
experience is blotted out when we awaken. So indeed, not
only are we responsible to ourselves and to our earthly commitments: we are in a constant and significant relationship
with our angel and other spiritual beings. We are sustained by
this other world; we are beholden to it. This world is all

around us; it only requires a change of consciousness, like falling asleep, and we are in it.

And further, we can ask what life is: a force which we derive from the unseen world. We of ourselves cannot be the authors of life: we can only be a channel through which life flows in us. Life itself remains a mystery, however much it is analysed and maybe synthesised by modern scientific methods. And life manifests in the body of life forces, known in spiritual science as the ether body, which surround and sustain our physical being.

Here we return to our theme: when we live with someone, especially when we sleep together, something changes in the ether body. The ether bodies of lovers begin to unite, to become attached to each other. A bonding takes place not only in our souls, as happens when we relate deeply and warmly with a friend. The practice of living together bonds our life forces. This is what is meant by St Paul when he speaks of 'becoming one flesh.' It is our life-bodies, not our fleshly bodies, that grow together.

This happens most actively through sexual intercourse. To have sex means giving the partner a part of one's life-body and taking a part away from that person. Casual sex is not so casual; it is not without consequences: the life body of someone who 'sleeps around' is torn to shreds. This can affect the stability of the soul in its power of thinking and its ability to exercise will. It also weakens the flow of feeling, undermining it with emotional sentiments: the soul life loses its purity, not only because of what might be deemed immoral behaviour, but also through the losing of the wholeness and wholesomeness of the etheric body. This is more particularly to be felt by women, who when they participate in love-making give themselves much more deeply than men. One could say that for a woman, sex is never casual.

The forces of life are especially active in sperm and ovum. They carry life each in their own way: they reflect the rhythms of the life-body and are affected by the arousal of the soul. The sperm is like a darting particle of dynamic light, eager for the egg which is a still body of warmth. When they unite and conception takes place, a soul and spirit being is drawn to the fertilized egg and begins to build a body for the eternal Self, which will have lived through many lives already, and now has accepted the father and mother, the giver of the sperm and egg, to be the parents that this soul-being needed to fulfil destiny and carry out the mission. This happening unites eternity with mortality, spirit with matter, destiny with a new earthly freedom, and heavenly bliss with the hardship of being on earth. This is a holy event approaching the same sublime level as the transubstantiation of bread and wine in the Eucharist.

This faculty of procreation, given to man and woman, asks for dedication and commitment; any misuse shatters its holiness. Compare the situation when two people make use of this privilege without making a commitment to each other, and when two people who are bonded in love for each other and recognize that they have a destiny together, jointly pledge to build their togetherness on a firm foundation of total and unconditional commitment to each other. In one case there is no vessel to hold the consequences of living together. In the other their commitment can constitute a marriage when it is witnessed by Man and God.

That is the essential meaning of marriage: the two who marry clearly state their pledge to each other before human witnesses, and before the spiritual world, through a service which calls on the spirit to unite with the couple and hallow their togetherness. This pledge is lifted up into the realm of the eternal, through prayer and ritual, and a covenant comes about: if the couple strive to support each other in their spiritual growth, the spiritual powers will accompany them and indeed present the marriage to the throne of God. Once this covenant is sealed in a sacrament, it will never dissolve: it becomes a spiritual entity, a living impulse, a force that never tires or loses interest.

If it then happens that the marriage becomes too difficult for the couple to maintain, which generally means that their relationship has gone awry, a court of law may dissolve the legal marriage: but this act of divorce does not dissolve the covenant that came into being at the sacred marriage of the couple. They may have to admit that they cannot live up to the aims and goals that they pledged themselves to strive for, that other forces or problems have intervened; but they cannot say that their covenant is dissolved or that their marriage has broken or died. For a spiritual entity does not die.

What then happens when two people who have married decide that they cannot uphold their marriage any longer, and they leave each other? Quite apart from the trauma that the children in the family suffer, there is suffering in the spirit as well. We can be quite specific, thanks to what is known through modern spiritual science. When a marriage is solemnized and the spiritual world sees it and unites with it, what happens is that an angelic being draws near to the couple and becomes the guardian of the community of life-forces and heart-intentions formed by the couple and the children who may be drawn towards them.

This being, like our own individual guardian angel, does not interfere with the free will of the couple: that would work against the furthering of individual responsibility, which belongs to fully authentic human beings. But this guardian being watches over the couple and (to use a modern term) processes their experiences. It is thanks to this caring by the spiritual world that a marriage develops its own dynamic and goes through a biography.

The angel can assist the marriage in a real way, for instance by bringing the couple into touch with people who can help them to grow and to cope with difficulties that crop up. On the other hand the angel may countenance hard times for the couple, because they need them for deepening their relationship. It is a common experience that when the couple are open the guide appears, as if by magic. This can be through the coming of a child who brings a specially testing problem to the couple, like a deformity or handicap. These provide the opportunity for growth in the marriage.

The angel of the marriage will also speak to the consciences of the couple, who may need to change an attitude. As the angel cannot direct but only work through grace, the couple do well to form an open connection to this being, so that such guidance and wisdom can flow to them.

We can be reminded of Christ's words in foretelling the Whitsun event: 'I will send you a counsellor.' By becoming more open to the nearness and helpful devotion of spiritual entities, partners in a marriage can become conscious that their marriage is of interest and of concern to the spiritual world. They will become aware of the unlimited resources of wisdom and love that can be drawn upon, to make their marriage fulfilling for themselves and beneficial to the world around.

In our time the beings of the spirit world respond to our calls for them to help us. But unless called they will not, they may not, intervene: except in instances of imminent danger, when the Christ or his messenger comes in the form of a helping friend to rescue the situation, and then disappears when the danger is over.

This knowledge of the helping angel, the spirit of a marriage community, can encourage us to see the value of a sacramental marriage which brings this covenant into being. It can also help us to realize what happens when a marriage can no longer be maintained by the couple. A difficult passage is no reason to stop the marriage, for such passages are the means whereby the couple can grow and change. But if the situation deteriorates so badly that the couple are breaking down each other's selfhood and a marriage counsellor is unable to help, then an end to the situation has to happen. This means a painful withdrawal of the angel who had connected with it. Just as human beings can initiate the call for help, so also those concerned need to send their thoughts to the angel, who is losing his means of working for mankind and has to experience a kind of bereavement. This may explain why a divorce, even if it ends what had become a dreadful marriage, is always a painful process: beside their own pain, the former couple possibly experience the pain of the Angel.

These considerations help us to realize that marriage as a sacrament cannot be entered into lightly. It needs preparation, so that the two who wish to marry become conscious of the undertaking they will make to each other.

The modern idea of marriage does not fit into the traditional church wedding. The standing of each individual and the equality of men and women need to be recognized. The image of the bride being 'given away,' and the promise to love, honour and obey, hardly fit to the thoughts and feelings of modern couples. The renewed sacrament of Marriage, as celebrated in The Christian Community, calls up the awareness of a special responsibility in those who marry: namely to strive for togetherness, one that embeds itself into life, into all that works through the biography and destiny of each partner. It also points to the spiritual dimension in the striving of both, so that the divine force in earthly life is acknowledged and itself can be a witness to the commitment that the two persons make to each other.

The modern marriage envisages that those who marry are not two halves making a whole but two wholes who place themselves in the service of each other. The aim is not only to share a domestic arrangement or even for the sake of bringing up a family; these aspects need a higher principle to enliven and safeguard them. This higher principle is one of regard for the wholeness of each other, the unfolding person who is equally at home in the spiritual world and in the earthly. Regard for the one who can aspire to great thoughts and enjoy a rich imagination, and at the same time can be fully practical and wise about earthly needs and situations that life presents. It calls for persons who are able and glad to give space to each other and enable the other to grow. Persons who know their own weaknesses and selfish habits and are working to overcome them. Persons who are striving in their soul life to be channels of feeling and love. Persons who have greatness of heart.

These qualities require an acceptance of the divine, the welcoming of an angelic guide, and the pledge to be aware of the wellbeing of one's partner. These components build a modern marriage, bonded in the love of the partners, which ensures that children born to them will have an emotionally and spiritually nurturing family life. They also make it possible for the couple to go through hardships, setbacks and difficulties in their individual biographies and their relationship without turning against each other: indeed they will be able to accept the challenges and learn through the experience of dealing with them openly and together. Then, as the children grow up and leave the home, the couple will continue to sustain and enrich each other's wholeness and prepare for the ageing process that can turn knowledge into wisdom and experience into understanding. They will look back over the decades of marriage and celebrate the blessings it has given them. As the end of life approaches, their spirituality will lead them on to face death as the culminating grace that dissolves our earthly limitations and welcomes us back to our true home.

# 21. The music of marriage

## *A wedding address*

'Dear Ursula and Peter ...'

... We have all witnessed your marriage and we contemplate its meaning. And now, in deepest inwardness, we unite our hearts and spirits in blessing your community of life.

Melody ... harmony ... rhythm ....

Relationship in a marriage is like a piece of music, and the partners in a marriage are the composers: they compose this music together.

For relationship needs a clear rhythm on which to build. Its melody will explore the new; you can never anticipate the way a melody is going, even if it repeats itself, for there is always development. In regard to harmony, sometimes there is dissonance — chords that are not in accord: but then, as the music develops, harmony is restored.

There are times when the relationship will be in slow movement — adagio. At other times it will be allegro: rippling along, enjoying each new moment, welcoming the new day and all that takes place in the course of it, and enjoying each other in the twirls and trills of soaring phrases. There are all possible moods in a relationship, as in music; all possible modes. What makes it like music is the unity, the wholeness and the working out of a theme.

Destiny has led you together, and there is a deep-down

meaning in your togetherness: this you have shown to one another and to your friends. You needed to meet; it was in your stars. But your marriage — your statement of 'Yes, I do' — this was a free deed. We were all witnesses to an existential moment of a high order. But above all it was witnessed by the beings of the spiritual world who are close to you, and by the Being who will safeguard your marriage. All these witnessed how you pledged to strive to do all in your power .... To do what? To care for each other? This wasn't mentioned. To be friends with each other? This is taken for granted. So what did you pledge? Let us explore the answer.

Marriage is an attempt at replacing a loss: that deep-down loss that makes us feel bereft and long for companionship, for community, for healing our incompleteness. What really makes us whole is to be united again with our true higher being. The predicament of mankind is that this true self stays in heaven when we each come down to earth, and only in fleeting moments of bliss and enlightenment do we feel that higher being to be near. And so we grieve. Our life is actually accompanied throughout by that feeling of bereavement, that sense of separation from our higher self: we long for that mystical marriage that will make us whole again. Through many ages human culture has led us to forget the true self so as to be content with being on earth, and to assuage our grief through searching for a spouse and marrying: the yin would search for the yang to make a whole. And of course there were good grounds for this because, through marriage, families could be founded and nurtured, children could find a secure setting in which to grow: and society sought to make marriages stable. The ideal was to live happily ever after with one's partner.

But we don't live in that kind of time any longer. From the beginning of this century we entered the Light Age, and it is gradually becoming more possible for us to meet and to know our own higher beings. The spiritual realities in which we live are no longer veiled in symbols or shrouded in dogma, but are becoming more tangible. Since the beginning of this century spiritual science has made it possible for each person to walk a path towards his own higher being: but it is a lonely path, and the modern person longs for a companion-on-the-way.

So marriage today is not only to share the life on earth and bring it comfort, but also to stimulate that search for one's own higher being. Because the other one believes in it and strives to know it. The modern partner in marriage says: I like you as you are, with your personality; I see its meaning and I feel a connection to it through destiny. But the most important gift that I can give to you is to believe in your own true self and never to let it fade from my mind. When life is tough and when you are feeling down, I will try by my very closeness to reassure you of your infinite value — to me, to the world and above all to yourself. And I know you will do the same for me.

Now we can hear, sounding gently from the spirit around us, a new music: the world rejoices over your commitment to relationship of this new kind: togetherness for life; a life full of melody as you explore the miracles and meet the tests of each new day. A life of harmony, as you follow the rules of good composition and translate passing discords into deeper concordance. And a life of rhythm: the underlying constant rhythm of your selfless love for each other. You will be challenged by much that is new and different, but this rhythm will always sustain you.

Marriage is new in our time. Not now the bonds that lead to bondage. Community of life in this new way, blessed through the renewed sacrament, is like music that soars high: music that opens the heavens and brings joy down to earth. And it offers back something very precious, that only life on earth can produce: human love.

## *Joy*

We enter marriage with joy: we feel there has been a victory of healing and companionship over separation and incompleteness. We celebrate the parts becoming a whole; we hope for a new spring of happiness to moisten our parched soul-landscape with its living water. We may feel the heavens rejoicing and souls descending to join our new community-of-life. We sense the courage-to-commit rising in us as we state our intention to strive for mutual love and companionship.

Marriage has to do with growing as a person. This means growing in those qualities that enhance companionship. Being considerate as well as resolute; being cheerful as well as earnest; being able to take in, listen and receive, as well as giving, directing and transcending oneself.

It is a school in self-knowledge; in giving space to another, and in knowing how to tune in. It offers no stage for a soloist who is unable to perform in harmony with others. It is a school of change, because it demands change in habits and challenges anything in one's make-up which is stuck.

But it is also a means to joy. There is a deep spiritual and religious principle that works between two people who are together in harmony: a third element draws near. This weaves a soul-tapestry of incredible worth, namely the power we have referred to as feeling in the earlier chapters of this book. Feeling, entering into a marriage, gives it an enriching link with the universal divine force. This breath of heaven, this spirit, expands the souls and fills them with warmth. When joy arises in a person, and more especially in a bonded couple, warmth of heart is stirred: there arises the impulse to praise; sorrow is dissolved into peace, and the mind opens to the good. When joy enters a marriage it helps the partners to be aware of the good forces at work in their lives. They will recognize the significant coincidences, the goodness in each other and in those around them, and the miracles that are happening daily. They will both more readily acknowledge the goodness in themselves, something otherwise so easily denied. They will know the value of making an effort to overcome lethargy and cramp. They will appreciate each other and feel appreciated. And their communication, both verbal and silent, will be a source of comfort and reassurance. With joy in their souls they can be open to the future and accept its mystery.

The classical Greeks called joy *khará:* the 'ah' sound predominates; first a breaking in of 'ah,' then it rolls on. Joy has something universal, total, complete. So it belongs to marriage, which opens the way towards wholeness, fulfilment and a working of heaven upon earth.

## Tension

The music of marriage contains tension as well as harmony. The very word 'intend' expresses the quality of the marriage bond: it has to do with stretching (as in 'tension' and 'tent'). There is strain, tautness, direction, a sense of purpose: it is a will-word, not merely an attitude. Without the attendant effort that is needed, it will fail. There has to be tension if there is movement and exhilaration: for a new creation is to come about. And every marriage is a new creation, continually in the making. Like with sailing a yacht, there has to be constant adjustment to the prevailing conditions, but also a clear sense of direction which can be maintained regardless of adverse winds. Indeed resistance can sharpen one's keenness to achieve an aim, and winning through becomes all the more real and satisfying.

As we develop our individualness we may find it more difficult to share the same space with another and to have that other person scrutinize our every action. The human being is complex and sensitive. Sharing life requires a wealth of tolerance, space-giving and respect: otherwise the joy of marriage can be upset, giving way to anguish, and then can follow aggression (even if only verbal) or withdrawal. Thereby a process is set in motion that undermines the togetherness and sends the couple into divergent dynamics.

Generally the man will withdraw; he will seek a safe place on his own in which to work out his emotional upset, away from those who would discuss and analyse his actions. Hence the reluctance of a man to submit himself to marital counselling or partnership work. He needs a sanctum, a bolt-hole, a cave, perhaps a workshop or a den, in which he can be by himself and 'come to himself.' If he is upset he will usually not want to discuss the state of his emotions with his wife. He has hurt pride, which causes him to feel insecure; the imp on his left shoulder screams at him, 'You've blown it!' He may appear furious, but deep down he is anxious: 'I have lost my self-esteem, my self-respect.'

The wife who is upset about some failing of her husband will want to stay with the problem, express her anguish and be listened to. Her anger is not because her husband is a blackguard; she has not married a blackguard, nor does she love one. She loves and has married her husband, her man. Now she feels this man is not living up to his own ideal, the ideal that she has seen, knows and loves with incredible loyalty. She is wrathful because of her disappointment in his behaviour, not living up to his true being, and holy wrath is akin to love. This is not something she can be silent about. If her husband runs to his bolt hole and disappears, or turns his aggression on her, her anguish is compounded: for her man has disappeared and his place is taken by a spectre of either a weakling or a monster.

## Resolving

There is the unknown part of ourselves; we may call it the unborn part. At times this exerts pressure on the conscious part, and this struggle within our own soul causes our malaise, our disquiet, and brings about a feeling of disharmony. This affects our relating to whoever shares our space. Our partner or our spouse can help us to establish our inner harmony by sensing that a process is going on within us and by being open to understand what is happening. If that companion is perceptive enough to see that a birth is taking place, a new quality of soul is being born, he or she will help the process through the power of love, through positive regard. But so often, because of the closeness of living together, and the insecurity lurking in the psyche of both partners, the disharmony is taken as a denial of the partnership, or at least as a questioning of its worth. And this hurts. And a person who is hurting easily reacts and thereby causes more hurt and more reaction.

Yet such upsets can be turned to the positive. Crises are opportunities for deepening, growing and expanding the soul. There has first to be a jointly felt awareness and acknowledgement of the upset. 'See, hold it: we are upset; let's work at it.' Both have to go through an inner process. This can at times be helpfully facilitated by a third person, although this should not be necessary.

The steps of the process are as follows:
1. Acknowledge the *upset* that is giving rise to *anguish*. It has caused a loss of peace of mind and harmony.
2. Examine your reaction: *anger, anxiety, aggression, shame* or *withdrawal*. It has caused a loss of communication.
3. Accept your *loneliness,* with the attendant fear and insecurity. It has caused a loss of mutual support.

Now has to begin your effort to help yourself by:
4. Turning loneliness into *solitude*. Be still and consider deeply what is happening.
5. Awaken to a new *revelation* coming from within you, as a consequence of all that is happening. Sense the elation that this brings about in your feeling soul.
6. Now go back to your spouse and *relate* what has stirred in you, and listen to her or him to hear what happened there.
7. *Celebrate* what is new, and admire the mystery of each other's being.

This way the upset releases its gift, and life's stresses take on meaning. But the upset is precarious, and it takes much coolness to work through it in this way. So it is good to engage in a process with one's partner or spouse that yields the same result in growth without requiring the thunderstorm or the turmoil.

A metamorphosis of the seven steps could be undertaken with each other at various times, regularly if possible, as a personal ritual leading to a celebration:
1. Take some time, safe from the risk of interruption, be

comfortable and at ease; clear the mind of pressures, worries and clutter, if necessary by talking out or writing down whatever would disturb the process.

2. Contemplate the Mystery of each other: *Who are you? Who am I?*

3. Let your *feeling* come alive and flow between you, remembering that feeling is not emotion but a universal radiation of love from the divine world, that yearns to include you in its flow.

4. Come to *solitude,* each within yourself. This is a preparation for the renewal of sharing. It means stillness, being alone, coming to oneself. Henri Nouwen writes: 'Just as words lose their power when they are not born out of silence, so openness loses its meaning when there is no ability to be closed.' Two pages later he writes: 'To live a spiritual life we must first find the courage to enter into the desert of our loneliness and to change it by gentle and persistent efforts into a garden of solitude. This requires not only courage but also a strong faith .... It is the movement from the restless sense to the restful spirit.'[16]

5. Out of the mood of peaceful stillness, *meet* your partner again. Re-kindle the intention of the moment of your commitment to each other. Remember the free deed that it was, and feel your freedom now to *meet* and *be met.*

6. Allow the holiness of this moment to fill you. You are like priests celebrating a mystery, the mystery of your togetherness.

7. Let your hearts be open, *relate,* en-joy the newness in your relating, the deepening and expanding that is taking place here and now. Celebrate it with a new intimacy of soul, by sharing a content from a book or a work of art, or a meal by yourselves, or in rest. Find the

way to seal the event and close it, before returning to the demands of everyday life. Here are words that you could use together to close the ritual:

We have listened, and have heard each other.
We have cleared our vision and have seen each other.
We have renewed our knowledge of each other.
We have confirmed our togetherness.

## Intervals

Solitude plays a vital part in the building and sustaining of a close and intimate relationship. Both of the processes outlined above turn on the achieving of a state of solitude. This is aloneness which has overcome the sadness of loneliness: it accepts what is, including oneself, and relates it to an element that is eternal.

'I am. It is. All is part of a living, weaving, growing whole. Let me listen to its music, savour its wisdom, feel its meaning.' In solitude the deeper realms of the soul can open and reveal truths that are otherwise safeguarded from our everyday chattering consciousness. In solitude I come to my Self.

A relationship that involves living together needs times of solitude; times when the pressure of sharing is laid aside and each partner can be alone. These periods of solitariness 'knit up the ravelled sleeve of care'; they restore us after a time of sharing, as sleep restores us after a day's activity. And indeed sleep is a question: must one always sleep together? We will come back to this.

*Re-lating:* the very prefix 're' indicates something repeated. A relationship of togetherness can live, breathe and grow only if it is rhythmical, with times of intimate sharing alternating with times of being on one's own. Our power of love is rhythmically impulsive. It is not a state of being: when it is alive and full of energy it resembles the arterial blood, bright red and pulsing round the system in tune with the beat of the heart. The trouble with most partnered relationships is that they more resemble the dull flow of venous blood, a murky purple in colour. Sure, the venous blood carries the dross of expended energy; oxygen has combusted into carbon dioxide. But on returning to the heart it is straight away despatched to the lungs to get rid of the dross and be renewed. So also a close relationship needs regular clearing and cleansing. There is too much combustion in living together for a couple to ignore the need for the lung factor: and this requires solitude in which both can renew their individual energies, and a ritual such as that described above to enable the relationship itself to be re-invigorated. How often we see relationships, especially marriages, that are venous and not arterial! Times together are essential, but also times apart.

Much of our daily renewal takes place in sleep. It is the apotheosis of solitude. It provides the lung-factor to our daily rhythm. But it does more than this. In going to sleep and in waking up we are intensely involved with our own Self. Indeed, esoterically viewed, it is at these moments of transition that we are most able, with persevering exercise, to be in touch with our Self. Yet the custom and expectation of marriage is that the partners sleep together in a shared bed. Naturally this has its reasons: deep reasons, no doubt. But if sleep is such a personal process, there is much to be said for having the alternative of sleeping alone, in a separate room, whenever either partner feels the need for solitude. Then sleeping together ceases to be a routine.

There is a valuable perception of how situations have a built-in dynamic, and relationships of wife and husband fol-

low this general course. A situation begins with the element
of *drama:* we are challenged by a new set of circumstances:
it is exciting and we do not know how it will work out; we
are on the alert to be fully conscious of all that is happening. After a while this dramatic state moves into one of *ritual:* we are more at ease; the rhythmic element sustains the
action, and meaning flows in to keep the process vital and
sacred. But if this is not kept alive it subsides into *routine.*
And this no longer contains vitality; it is assailed by same-
ness: there is less and less need to be conscious of what is
happening, and we think we can rely on the situation continuing for all time. Which of course does not happen. What
ensues is a new phase of *drama!*

So, in a marriage, the sacred rituals begin to lose their
meaning if the couple move from ritual to routine. To keep
ritual alive requires the constant renewal of consciousness,
which means letting today be today, and not a rehash of yesterday. Routine contains seeds of destruction. Real music is
dramatic in the best sense, or has the quality of ritual; the
music of marriage requires this too. Routine is beat: like the
drone of a motor, mechanical and monotonous. Ritual is
rhythmical: the matrix may remain the same but each celebration is infused with new spiritual input. Drama is at the
cutting edge, the zone of discovery.

Where do you wish your marriage to be? Where is it now?

## Crescendo

A composer provides a channel for the inflow of musical
inspiration. A marriage is like the unfolding of a piece of
music: the couple join forces to provide a channel for the
inflow of destiny. Marriage is the prime instrument of destiny: its form and its openness allow for 'new' things to

happen. It is karma that initially sets the scene for things to happen: some past-life event backgrounds the new occurrence. And undoubtedly it is through karma that the would-be partners meet. But do they therefore have to become partners? Karma cannot make anyone do anything: it provides circumstances; it engenders feelings of attraction and attachment, or likewise of antipathy. But what we make of the given situation and the given feelings is up to us. So whether or not these feelings should impel us to marry is a question: it is not possible to form a lasting community of togetherness, purely on the basis of recognition of a karmic connection.

Karma cannot call for marriage, cohabitation, or engagement in a sexual relationship. These can only be true and free if they are graced by energy that comes out of the future: revelation, exploration, the building of the new. To marry because of karma could be like plunging into a phase of routine from which there is no escape. So if you want to marry someone because you share the conviction that you were monks together in the middle ages, beware! Celebrate your shared memories in other ways, but don't feel that the attachment is destined to lead to marriage.

 Marriage needs to be based on a love that is free. Free to lead you both to new heights in your path towards individual growth. And inward growth has to do with growth-in-love. Growing: crescendo. Hence the crescendo in marriage.

Destiny indeed plays a part in a marriage, but it is good to remember that marriage is more than this. You have, in your marriage, the means to shape a large part of your life out of the freedom of love. Whilst so much of your daily existence with home, husband or wife and family, is seemingly fixed in routine, every element in it can be enlivened through a conscious dedication. 'I have to do this, but it is part of what I have chosen out of freedom, and so every act of mine in response to the situation I am in is connected to that free deed. What I do now can be a freely accepted necessity, and so acquire the quality of a deed done in love.'

Then I work out of my heart, and the heart never gets tired. Moreover, spiritual science tells us that a deed done in love does not carry karmic consequences. So by working out of love I make myself a free person, even in this wider sense. Marriage is therefore a special school in freedom.

## Development

Much of our relating to one another is unconscious: we speak of falling in love, of being swept off our feet, of finding ourselves in the clouds. Such is the impact of romantic love, as a force that rushes into our souls and proceeds to take over, warming all our attitudes and ideals, though perhaps also overwhelming our rationality. We find ourselves in effect of love. But it is well known that this kind of love does not last: it may be dramatic, but it seldom translates into ritual unless it is transformed.

Then there is the more general sense of sympathy for certain people and things. We like a person; we like a work of art. Maybe this positive feeling is instinctive, or it grows with our knowledge and understanding of that person or thing. It is a sentiment that arises in us. We do not create these forms of love. We may create the conditions for them and open a space: but they arise in us somewhat unconsciously. As do our affinities to our blood relations. They are part of our legacy from the past.

But there is also new love: this introduces a new motif in the symphony. This is the product of our own free endeavour. It is to the old love as sunlight is to moonlight: it is present, vibrant, creative and sustaining; not a reflection, not passive. It can only come about through relating between ego-endowed beings; it cannot come about from hereditary or blood-tie groupings. It comes through the twin actions of comforting and confronting one another as individuals. If we first know ourselves as individuals, free and authentic, we are then able to enter consciously into a relationship, an intentional community, with others. Along this channel can flow our interest in the other, our positive regard, our concern for his or her well-being and right-growing.

This power of love and compassion, freed from blood-bonds, was brought into the world by Gautama Buddha. It prepared the way for the mission of Christ Jesus six centuries later; and the impact of Christ's work and his working on since his incarnation is still far from being fully recognized. His mission was to take the deed of Buddha from the sphere of soul into the sphere of life forces: in other words to bring love a stage deeper, as a prelude to the next phase, when it can work as a transformative power into the earth itself.

Thereby the earth, despite its littleness, could engender a new power that would in time transform the whole universe, namely the power of human love. Divine love had created the universe, but in man it could only manifest as love that is less than conscious. What will make the difference in our time is the generating within free human beings of a new power, impelled by the creative potential of human Selves, that is unencumbered by remnants of an instinctive affinity.

Christ showed that the old ways of love have to be replaced by new. He took Peter and Andrew, and the sons of Zebedee, away from their fathers; he spoke about forsaking of mother and brother. He cursed the fig tree because it symbolized a way of spiritual development that worked unconsciously.

He initiated a process that leads human beings out of the matrix of inherited relationships, with their unconscious, un-worked-for affinities, into a new nexus of freely-created relationships, that can be sustained only with ongoing effort. These are not rooted in the past; their life-forces are continually regenerated out of the future, through the sun-power of the Christ-Being himself.

Love becomes transcendent, immediate, vibrant, though at the same time precarious. Such human beings rise to the stature of co-creators and co-healers; they become like Christ to all other human beings, as channels of divine power which they regenerate out of human freedom and learn to direct and bestow on their companions, free of inherited affinities but out of recognition of the spiritual truth and worth of every person.

The quest for this new love can involve us all. The ideal schooling for it is found in the modern marriage: a freely-sustained togetherness of a man and a woman for the sake of each other's spiritual growth, their security and enjoyment of daily life, and the well-being of their children. A living cell that can generate new love within itself and let it resound beyond into the wider social community, as a music that conveys an ongoing healing and blessing.

## Finale

We can no longer expect to be enveloped in love. Warmth in relationship, affection and affinity are no longer given to us as part of our nature. Some instinctive urges to nurture and protect are still found in human beings, especially in those who remain embedded in tribes and clans and

large extended families. But with the growth of consciousness and the freeing of blood bonds, each person is
increasingly alone and has to come to terms with this feeling of isolation.

Even marriage is no cure for loneliness. We have to
accept the painful fact: marriage can no longer take away
the feeling of being alone. This is not because marriage
has failed; it is because the human being has changed.

 The traditional idea of marriage has been unable to keep
up with the pace of human evolution. The modern West-
erner can no longer be satisfied with the kind of marriage
that satisfied our grandparents and great-grandparents, or
even our parents: for the rate of change in our present time
far outstrips the rate in any age till now.

So if man is changing, marriage has also to change.
This has to do with the dynamics of love; these have been
going through a metamorphosis ever since Christ changed
the water into wine at the marriage of Cana. Already there
the old bonding had run out. That which brought about a
warm feeling between people, and was a necessary lubri-
cant for human relating in general and marriage in particular, had run out. This expressed itself symbolically when
the wine ran out at the wedding. It was clearly up to Jesus
Christ, newly emerging as a spiritual leader, to remedy the
immediate situation and avert a dreadful predicament: but
this very necessity opened the way for a breakthrough in
the dynamics of love.

His mother gave him more than encouragement. Something was working between them which he recognized as
the power of her womanhood, and he acknowledges this in
addressing her as 'Woman.' This word has baffled many
translators, as it seems to imply disrespect, but there is no
indication of this. He addressed the universal in her, her
essential nature, her fullest potential. 'Alone I cannot yet act;

this requires the co-working of womanhood.' Mary could then show the task and the privilege of Woman, the Woman in all of us, to affirm and empower, so that the Man in us can act. Jesus then acted, and in his deed he transcended the limitations of the past and drew from the future. She simply said to the attendants 'Do whatever he tells you.' Once again there was an immediate need, but something greater in the background. Mary, as one of the wedding-organizers, had to authorize the servants to accept the instructions of someone who was there only as a guest: but through this she opened the way for the manifestation of a miracle. And then the sign took place, Christ's first sign. He brought about the new wine, the new love.

The Gospel of John is more than narrative: it is written in a mystery language that can be taken deeper and deeper as we meditate on it. Here is a marriage: it is archetypal, otherwise it would not have featured in the Gospel. In the course of the marriage event something new needed to be introduced, indeed created: new wine, the best wine. That which brings about the feeling of cheerful togetherness, the feeling that we are all somehow one family, united by our common ties of blood, is no longer relevant. That which bonds us has to be created anew out of the life-carrying element of pure water. And it has to contain the blessing, the power, of the I am: the Ego, that is the new principle of the human being, the Christ-in-us.

This spiritual entity needs now to take hold of our individual selves: the sun-power in each human being has now to throw off the moon element of unconscious relating and bonding, the forming of families and clans out of the stream of heredity. This new individualness, this creative spark of sun-power that has been available to us ever since the creation of the new wine, has to become the source of strength in love. We are no longer endowed with love: it has to be drawn into ourselves, here and now and at all times by all human beings.

This was an immense challenge: it needed time; much else had first to happen. And meanwhile human relating has remained largely unconscious and moon-like; we resort to props and surrogates to maintain our sense of belonging and affinity. Loneliness threatens on all sides. Marriage, so long regarded as a cure-all, has lost the power to overcome loneliness. So we break down our marriages and try to build new ones, or deny the value of marriage altogether. Yet the weakness lies not in marriage. The idea that friendship can lead to commitment and that this can maintain itself and sustain couples through life is not a weak one; it is tremendously strong. Provided it is pulsated through and through with new wine, Ego-created, Self-sustained, Sun-powered new love.

In the two millennia since the marriage of Cana, the full reality of this event has been gradually sinking into human consciousness. Now, as the event enters its third millennium, there stirs the urge to become true bearers of a new wisdom of man. The sense of self is awakening. From this can develop authentic, self-powered love. Individuals will become responsible for their own lives and able to build community.

# 22. Difficulties and challenges

Two worlds come together when a man and a woman marry. Two different worlds. The man's world is not really as a woman believes it to be; nor is a woman's what a man thinks it is. It will take time for them to grow together. So it is vital to set out on your voyage of discovery with an open mind, ready to find what you never expected and to rejoice at the truth, beauty and goodness that lives in your partner's world.

## *Out to change the partner*

Men may imagine they have the task, even the duty, to tame their wives: to ensure that they know their place and what is expected of them. And Women may bask in the belief that their men will change their ways once they are married. The first courts failure; the second is an illusion. Both betray the attitude of being in possession of the other. This kind of love tries to control, without allowing a process of growth in the other. Love should help the partner to find freedom, not cause constriction. 'I will accompany you through your trials but will not take them away from you. I will be frank with you, but I will not deny your ability to care for yourself: I will leave you free to make your decisions and form your own resolves about your attitudes and your behaviour. I will listen to you, but I will not always agree with what you say or what you do.'

Keeping in mind the real essence of your partner, and trusting that the right guidance will come even when that true being is clouded over, will open up a space-for-growth and enable the partner to take responsibility for the process that is needed.

These problems can be largely averted if the marriage is prepared by pastoral counselling. The old custom of at least half a year of engagement and preparation has much to be said for it: this is especially so for a sacramental wedding.

During this time of preparing the couple can ask themselves if they have attitudes that could undermine the joy of being together. For instance snoring, inability to keep clothes tidy, poor habits in hygiene, hogging the bathroom, being fussy with food, uncouth eating manners, sniffing, raucous coughing, wanting the radio as a background noise, insisting on having the last word, being either stingy or spendthrift, being a poor listener, being sarcastic, running the partner down in company, given to jokes that mock and sting, having insatiable curiosity.

The chances of two people being a good fit right from the beginning are small; it is a matter of entering a flow and working at change together. But there has to be readiness to change on the part of both partners, especially in the seemingly insignificant habits that can irritate beyond measure. Without this the one who suffers may well start thinking: 'Better to be alone than to be irritatingly accompanied!'

There are more questions to explore before making a life-commitment:

Are we going to be rivals in our professional work? Will we compete for honours before our friends?

How similar are we, and how complementary? What aptitudes or qualities do we not cover between us?

What are our respective attitudes to money? What does each of us consider as luxuries?

Do our idiosyncrasies grate on each other?

Do we share attitudes, or accept each other's attitudes, to health foods, meat-eating, coffee, smoking, having friends round who stay late?

Can we appreciate each other's relatives and friends? Does one of us feel swamped by the other's overwhelming family?

Do we share a similar concern for safeguarding the environment (avoiding the use of poison sprays and of detergents that are not biodegradable, and abstaining from the burning of plastic in the incinerator)?

Do we agree about, or at least have an open positive regard for, each other's:

— religious beliefs and practices?
— political affiliations or inclinations?
— love for classical, light or pop music?
— enjoyment of silence for concentrated reading?

Do we like the same kind of drama or film?

— have the same attitude to television?
— like the same kind of people, and admire the same kinds of feats or achievements?
— have compatible attitudes towards racial or cultural prejudices?

Are we well attuned in regard to love-making and sex?

Perfect fits are rare, and possibly boring: but in preparing for a commitment to share life, it is valuable to work through questions like these. They are all aspects that will be relevant in the process of building a truly intimate relationship. It is not so much a matter of being alike in all these respects, but of accepting what is not alike in the partner's way of life.

## *The first pregnancy*

A young marriage usually begins with a romantic time, when the physical relations are important and fulfilling; and then the wife becomes pregnant, and the coming child makes everything look different. She is now more volatile in her moods, and her thoughts are centred on motherhood. Her husband has two reactions (at least). The one is to feel rather proud: he is going to be a father, and he begins to imagine how his life will change and be enriched by the coming of the child and the founding of his own family: he has noticed how his friends at work all made a step in their maturity when they became fathers. He has become aware how a certain inner peace arises: and the feeling stirs 'I will have achieved something, and nobody can take that achievement away from me.'

And yet the other reaction that a prospective father will have is 'Gee, this is a responsibility: we'll have to start doing sums; it's going to be tough. It's goodbye to our second breadwinner, for a while at least.' And so he sets out to earn more by getting advancement or by obtaining better qualifications. He decides to take an evening-class course to improve his professional standing or in some way upgrade his career-prospects. Or else he prepares himself to work extra hours, to take on more responsibility, to run risks; he may seek to change his job so as to get a higher salary. All this so that he can better support his coming family. One way or another, he has to rise to the new demand. So it becomes a time of stress for the husband, and he devotes more of his energies to his work, to the progress of his career, to what has to be done.

This is an unfortunate synchrony, because the wife has reached the point of needing more of caring and stable companionship just at the time when the husband may become less able to give this to her. She will soon have to give up her work and remain at home all day; she is not sleeping so well, or she is suffering from early-morning sickness or other ailments that make life uncomfortable; and gradually she becomes heavy and less agile. She is brooding over her coming child and wondering 'What will happen if it's handicapped?' Or 'Will it be a nervy child?' She knows that first children are often nervy. 'How will I manage the birth? I'm a bit scared: is it going to be stressful?' All these anxieties make her more vulnerable than usual, and greatly dependent on her husband as her anchorage in life. He is the companion, the support, the one she loves and who loves her, the one for whom she is doing all this, who has fathered the coming child: the one who is going to be the head of the family this child will initiate, the one who gives meaning and purpose to her whole existence and makes worthwhile and joyful all the cleaning and housekeeping, all the pains and worries of impending motherhood. She wants to share with him her excitement. She would like to show him the many things that she is getting ready: the cradle and the baby blankets, and the bootees she has started to knit. It would be so natural to open the package with him: 'Look at these nappies that I bought today!' But it is suddenly too difficult: communication between them is under stress. Gone is the togetherness of theatres and concerts and the sharing of daily work-experience: she has to focus on motherhood, and this is a strange scene for him.

What had begun with love now ends with 'poor me' for both of them.

The life of a young couple is fraught with such stress-points.

## *Crisis at twenty-eight*

When a couple set out on their married life in <u>the developmental time of the twenties</u>, there can be a critical phase in the emotional life when one partner reaches the age of twenty-seven to twenty-eight. Youth comes to an end (sometimes suddenly) and buoyancy subsides; he or she feels hopelessly inadequate: 'Where has my courage gone? My energy's not what it was: I seem to be getting old already, I was on top of the world a couple of years ago, and now I am caught in a downswing.'

This is painful; it makes the person become introspective: 'What is the matter with my life now? I'm just not doing so well. There used to be so much in me I could depend on, and now that's all gone and I feel uncomfortably shaky. I can't even feel sure that my partner still loves me: I seem to have lost all support and openness and understanding. Worst of all, I don't seem to trust myself any more.'

But the picture looks different on another level. Our guardian angel who had accompanied us during our first twenty-seven years, is now withdrawing for a while. He has to leave us alone at this time, so that we can take a stronger hold on our life.

If we have some insight into what is happening, or if we receive good counsel, we know that this phase will pass quite soon. <u>It comes upon us in the guise of a malaise which is far from pleasant and is even scary to begin with</u>.

We can be reminded of a seven-year-old getting measles or a fourteen-year-old going through puberty. At each seven-year threshold one steps out of a sheath into greater freedom. So also at twenty-one: this is recognized as an important age.

At twenty-eight there comes another threshold, hardly celebrated and often much more of an inward challenge. The twenty-eighth year heralds a crisis that has to be handled with courage, trust, faith and above all acceptance of oneself. Until we are twenty-seven we can draw on the forces of youth: channels of energy and thought-strength are open to us; vitality and initiative, buoyancy and joy are our natural heritage. All this supplies our daily needs. Understandably we assume that this belongs to life; we don't realize that this natural endowment only lasts for the time of our youth. When we approach twenty-eight we must start to rely on our own inner resources: if we have the needed qualities of courage, trust, faith and acceptance of ourselves, we can manage the transition without difficulty.

Maybe in earlier times this transition happened so naturally that it was scarcely noticed. It has become a problem in our age because the resources called for to handle it are often sadly lacking. Especially lacking is acceptance of oneself. Every person needs to know 'I am somebody; I am worthwhile:' but this certainly is not a feature of our time; 'poor me' has become all too common. Before twenty-eight we can draw on our natural endowment; from then on everything depends on ourselves. If we have no sense of our own worth we can be shaken by the knock.

And now imagine that a couple is already married when this crisis comes. Perhaps the wife is younger and still youthfully exuberant, full of vigour and bounce, even somewhat intolerant and insensitive. And then the husband goes through this phase. He suddenly feels feeble, and is sure his wife also thinks he is feeble. He sees himself through her eyes and asks himself 'is she disappointed?'

The situation is not so different if the husband is in his thirties and his wife is coming up to twenty-eight. He begins to feel disappointed with her: he has forgotten his own twenty-eighth year and can't understand why she isn't giving him the full-on love she used to give. It is much the same either way, whether it's the husband or the wife who is going through the crisis, and whether or not the partner has already been through it. Either way there is need for support. The person at this threshold feels vulnerable, and the empathetic regard of the spouse can make all the difference.

If one accepts what is happening as a stage of development, with all the pain that it engenders, and if one seeks to understand it and to tackle it out of inner resources, there will be growth. If such resources are lacking, the person may fall prey to some easy way out: there are tempting anodynes to quell the ache within, and distractions are available everywhere.

People who use these means may indeed escape the pain: such outer supports can buoy them up and help them to float through the threshold as though they were in a dream. But they miss out on a developmental process, and an important opportunity for growing is lost. Through this they become a burden on themselves and on the world around. Such people are sadly typical of an age that has lost its natural instincts and has not yet gained the insight that can take their place.

# 23. From rapture to rupture

'Till death us do part.' For generations these words have stood over married couples like a reassurance or a threat. Is it a commitment for life, or a life sentence? Is it reasonable to promise into a far-distant future, when we cannot foretell the circumstances that may alter the ground on which our marriage has been based? So much can change, and surely will change.

These words do not occur in the marriage ritual of The Christian Community: this new ritual does not ask for such a promise. It speaks of intention, resolve; of fulfilling two spiritual roles, one for the man and the other for the woman. These roles have to do with being open to the sustaining power of resurrection, of enlivening and continually transforming their togetherness, so that they grow both in themselves and as partners to each other. The man is enjoined to bring the light of resurrection to the woman, letting it shine through him. The woman is called upon to 'go in her fullness' with the man (in German *folgen,* which revives the original meaning of *voll gehen); the fullness of her soul as a woman contains the light of resurrection, a deep theme of new Christology.

This approach can enable us to understand 'till death us do part' in the modern light of the dynamics of biography. Our life is never a straight-line progression. It is like an eddying stream with vortices forming as the water hits the rocks and dances round them, following the bends and hollows in the path of the stream. Always adjusting, moving forward in the main but in places being caught in the stagnation of a backwater. So is life. And the biography of a marriage is also fraught with vortices, eddying and stagnant times. Like the water-forms in a stream, marriage is an ever-changing pattern of dying and becoming.

It can happen that the relationship between the partners in a marriage dies. This can make it necessary to part: for if there is no hope for resurrection, to continue means breaking each other down. When this threatens, then, sadly, we have to recognize that for the couple the marriage is no longer sustainable.

'Till death us do part,' therefore, does not only refer to the ultimate death of the body. It can also refer to the death of our resolve or ability to maintain the close, intimate relationship of life-sharing.

There will be those who will regard this view as contrary to the ideal of a single partner for life. Undoubtedly this remains the ideal and the aim: every divorce is tragic and painful. No effort should be spared to come through to a resurrection of the love-relationship that once graced the marriage. But maybe it was based on a romantic attachment at a time when the couple did not have the maturity or the inner strength to make a real commitment. In our age of individualism, the structures of family, folk and society do not provide the support they once did: so we have to accept that people make mistakes in their choice of partners, or themselves change so much over the years that the context of their marriage erodes.

We have already touched on the pain that such a withdrawal from a spiritually blessed marriage can cause: the bonding angel has to withdraw. It is in the nature of spiritual dynamics in our present phase of evolution that the spiritual beings who guard us, the angels and the hierarchies, have to leave us free to make our own experiences. We have to make the decisions, while they suffer the consequences.

So there are breakdowns in marriages; there is divorce. No amount of denial will change this painful fact. But we can work on processes that strengthen marriages. Required would be:

— greater care in entering into marriage.
— the striving of both partners to grow with the marriage.
— an honest appraisal of the possible causes of break-down of a marriage, shared in openness.

## Entering into a marriage

Is our attraction for each other a sufficient basis for marriage?

Are we being forced into it?

Do we understand the dynamics of love? Romantic, sexual, committed.

Are we prepared for difficult times that will surely come? Illness, financial upsets, carrying each other's negatives, ageing. Boredom, burn-out. Crises of mid-life and middle-age; the years of declining powers, and so on.

Have we looked in depth at our own and each other's weak points when under stress? Can we cope with them?

Do we intend to grow as persons and as partners?

## The striving to grow in the marriage

Are we embarking on a programme of growth for our marriage? A growth in our power to understand and respect each other:

— in our ability to clear our own soul-clutter as life pro-
  gresses
— in communication
— in the setting of our aims and the steps to achieve
  them?

Are we prepared to share everything, especially that
  which lives in us as fear, shame and anger?

Are we able to widen our own self-regarding to include
  our partner and our children?

Are we prepared for the situations and attitudes that can
  jeopardize a marriage?

## Possible causes of breakdown

Here are some of the regular causes of marital breakdowns:

1. Since we married our times of sharing and listening
   to each other have dwindled to virtually nothing. It is
   rare for us just to sit together and talk.
2. Even when there is time, we seem unable to communicate our deeper feelings (especially the husband).
3. We are losing interest in each other. The body is
   familiar, the habits stale and rather irritating. The
   sparkle has gone out of our lives.
4. Our sexual life has no drama, nor ritual; only routine.
5. We are angry, or anxious. How are our anger, our
   fear? Are we covering them up while they gnaw
   away at us inside?
6. We no longer honour the agreements we made when
   we committed ourselves to each other. (This is especially relevant in second marriages that involve the
   caring for step-children. The new mother is often
   expected to cope with very complicated dynamics,

while the man goes to his den. This even if the husband had promised to play a full part in being with the children.)

7. Subtle rejection of each other is creeping into our daily existence. A distancing from what the other holds as valuable.

8. We are neglecting to nurture our marriage by sharing our ideas and interests, our enthusiasms and experiences.

9. Resentments, originally suppressed, now begin to surface. Like the fact that we decided to marry because of a pregnancy that was not wished for at the time. Or that your family never really thought I was good enough for you and appropriate for them.

10. Our marriage is mortally wounded because one of us has had an affair.

11. I used to idolize you; now that I know you better I can no longer do this.

12. I cannot cope with your swings of mood, or general moodiness; I never know where I stand with you.

13. What you find interesting leaves me cold.

14. You don't seem to be interested in who I really am.

15. I had such an unhappy childhood; it's all coming back to me now. I cannot trust any more: not even you, when you say you love me. Moreover, I need to hang onto my problem of feeling rejected at every turn; I like feeling sorry for myself.

16. *She*: I am never sure what role you expect me to fulfil: wife, mother, sex object, counsellor, housekeeper, nursemaid, doormat; your expectations change all the time, and you resent me if I get it wrong.

17. *He*: I am afraid to leave you: I doubt if you will manage and I'll feel guilty. Does that mean we've got to keep going in spite of our growing estrangement?

18. *Both:* I am afraid to let you go: I will not cope on my own.
19. You disempower me.
20. I have lost confidence in my worthiness to be loved.
21. You nag at me constantly.
22. I cannot just live for myself (guilt) and I cannot just live for you (antipathy, jealousy).

## *Unfaithfulness*

A marriage can go into turmoil when one spouse finds out that the other is carrying on an intimate relationship with another person. It happens often, and frequently breaks the marriage. What causes it? What can heal it?

It is usual to condemn the unfaithfulness of a partner in a marriage; the other partner is hurt, betrayed, cheated and rejected. These feelings go very deep: they shatter the basic trust in life. However, before piling on the condemnation it is valuable to remember that the partner who is hurt may well have to share the blame. It is unlikely that a person whose marriage is cheerful and fulfilling will seek a sexual relationship outside the marriage. If communication and mutual regard are waning, a hunger for new intimacy may well arise, even if it is seen as a casual 'fix' and in no way the starting of a rival relationship. Usually a man engages in affairs due to a mixture of situations: he may want to escape from a sense of inadequacy due to mid-life or middle-age crisis; he may feel that his romantic (sexual) life with his wife is going stale, and he would like to prove himself to himself. He may feel insecure in his career, or in other ways: he feels the need to break out. These reasons have to do with malaise with himself and wanting to sustain his self-image. 'See: I am still romantic, attractive, young' — and it is himself he is trying to convince. Or else he has an unsolved resentment against his wife, possibly because she knows his weaknesses too well and he feels vulnerable with her. A new partner will not hold up the mirror so candidly.

There is a further possible 'reason,' which may sound rather psychological but is worth considering. Jung held that every man has his masculine soul, or personality, his animus, which is his dominant mode; but that he also has his feminine side, his anima, which lies somewhat dormant until it is ready to emerge and some favourable event or happening brings this about. Because a man's animus is one-sided, his initial search for a partner makes him look for one who will complement him with 'otherness': so a man tends to marry a woman who has different talents from himself.

Then, in later years, roughly between forty-five and fifty-five, he feels the stir of the anima within him; this makes him respond ecstatically to a younger woman who is a feminine counterpart to himself: he falls in love; she is the one who really reflects back all that is in his anima. She is not a threat to his masculinity; indeed she harmonizes with it. This young woman is overwhelmed and possibly enticed by his effusive attention. He suddenly has powerful feelings stirring from depths in himself that he did not know existed. It is his renaissance, and he suddenly becomes a young Florentine.

Meanwhile he draws the young woman into his demanding network, with all the problems of an illicit affair: until, generally thanks to her innate sense of propriety and the attitude of her family and friends, the relationship shatters, leaving the man dumped on the shore. Perhaps it is only then that he begins to wonder what all this had been about. But then he realizes: this younger person was for him only a symbol, a personification, of his own nascent anima. Through the encounter this has now been born and can begin to manifest as a new aspect of his personal make-up. His thinking becomes more 'right-brained,' his heart warmer, his generosity more free. He has come through all this, unaware of the risk he was taking. Now he realizes how fortunate he is with his wife and family: they might well have thrown him out because of his blatant and embarrassing adventure. He is now perhaps a wiser, even humbler person, with a more all-round and balanced personality. But he has repair work to do, with his marriage, with his wife, and with himself. This scenario shows, though, just how self-regarding a man often can be. The young woman herself will not emerge unscathed and will need her own healing.

Many times such an affair leads to divorce, and he marries the younger woman and has a new family: it can go well. But the first wife remains wounded and mystified by the strange, unwarranted turn of fate, and the children inevitably suffer deeply.

A woman's approach to marriage may be very different from a man's. For her the commitment can be total, and she focuses her love onto the man who offered her security, fulfilment and also love. She sacrifices so much for him, but it is not seen as any kind of forgoing or limitation. Marriage for her is a ground on which a full life can be built, a life of nurturing and giving, and also of receiving and growing. It used to be said 'A man gets married; a woman marries.' Nowadays women are more liberated and build an alternative base for their life out of their profession, career and interests. So their expectations from a marriage, from a man, are less naive and all-trusting than they were some generations ago: but even now the young woman entering a marriage does so with high expectations and a preparedness to give. So if her marriage is seemingly intact she is less likely to indulge in affairs outside it than a man. Her view on life does not relish unfaithfulness. That is why it is so painful and perplexing for a wife to know of her husband's roaming and cheating. Unless, of course, the couple have taken all things into consideration and accept other liaisons as part of a style of life which is free of restrictions, possessiveness, suspicion and insecurity. But is this a marriage?

And yet there is always a mystery surrounding an act of unfaithfulness. It cannot be judged so easily. Who can really know? The guilty one will have been driven by various motives, needs and longings, and no-one else can possibly know what these were or how strongly they worked. No-one can know, which means no-one can judge: at best an empathetic counsellor can help towards a clearer understanding. But no-one, not even the hurt spouse, can really know: for no person can experience another person's experience. This we need to recognize when we wish to throw the first stone.

## Healing

Can there be forgiving? Can unfaithfulness be turned to the good, so that the marriage even benefits? An event like this gives the marriage partners a jolt: this is inevitable; the former pattern is shaken. Maybe the marriage had taken on the mode of routine, and now drama sweeps in. What is needed to restore the marriage and to reassure the wounded partner is firstly that the partners speak to each other, opening their hearts and listening to the feelings that maybe can now be expressed for the first time. Both partners are in crisis, and so is the marriage. Once the emotions really flow, tensions will work themselves out and moments of honesty, of being real, can occur. This sharing may need the assistance of a third person, skilled in counselling. Both partners would be feeling alone and lost. The sense of rejection and abandonment of the one party, the frustration and maybe guilt of the other, plus anger and fear in both, will inevitably arouse memories, possibly long buried in the subconscious. The normal buoyancy of childhood is inevitably injured by some experiences of rejection, guilt and frustration. Such suppressed pain and shame may be uncovered in the anguish of meeting one another after a 'betrayal.' Maybe what comes out is something that each has kept back from the other: this was a betrayal too. Yet something positive now emerges. Betrayal can only happen when there has been mutual trust and both have become vulnerable to losing that trust. It shows tenderness.

The next step is to recall and then renew or replace the covenant, the basic agreement, which the partners made to each other when they first came together. Maybe there was no clear agreement, only wishful thinking that accompanied the euphoria of romantic bliss: 'this will surely last forever, and no-one could possibly take your place.' So can this covenant be renewed? Or maybe a new covenant is now needed, that reflects the present hopes and aspirations of the couple. The wounded partner may claim more independence in the marriage, resolving to be less emotionally dependent on the other. Or the one who has 'sinned' may need to find a new meaning in life. In reviewing their lives together and sharing their feelings, the couple could do well to ask themselves what has really caused this upset?

Were there losses in earlier life, affecting one or both of them, that have not been properly grieved over? For instance the death of a child, or some shock that has not been worked through? These events could lie decades before, and now an event occurs that touches on the suppressed memory, plunging one or both partners into a depression. The cause remained unconscious because it was not understood at the time.

There are also rhythms in human biography that can herald sudden changes in mood, aspiration and buoyancy. The so-called 'moon node' takes 18 years, 7 months and 11 days, so the second moon-node (around 37 years and 3 months) and the third (about 55 years and 10 months) have a similar importance. A moon-node can be a critical time, ushering in a short period of uncertainty, or of more erratic moods: and maybe this explains the affair. They are problematic times: one is tempted to strike out against routine and the established order in one's life. But they are potential turning-points in biography, which can usher in new beginnings.

Once there has been an attempt, from both sides, to uncover the causes of the unfaithfulness, the next step is remorse, forgiving and reconciliation. If the review of the events surrounding the happening has been honest and open, the plea for forgiveness will not just be one way. So also, therefore, the forgiving. The act of pardoning has to remain close to the hurts and bitterness, the damage caused by the lapse: it has to be in that context. Forgiving is hard work, and implies rooting out the poisons and tensions that the wounding caused. Forgiving is a spiritual deed, requiring spiritual help, and calls for prayer, meditation and ritual. Forgiving makes a person vulnerable.

For the accusation has to stop, and this happens only when the accuser as well as the accused realize that they are covering up some weakness or guilt which has remained unrecognized. To form or re-form community requires each participant to admit weakness. Community is based on the admitted weaknesses of its members. If the couple wish to reconcile, to re-form their community, both need to drop all self-righteousness. They have to meet on a level.

We cannot go fully into forgiving: good work has been done on this subject. For instance in books by Paul Coleman and Sergei Prokofieff.[17]

## *Divorce*

When can one decide that the marriage is ruptured beyond repair?

— when forgiving no longer works, and bitterness refuses to dissolve.
— when the partners deny each other's worth and see only each other's dark side.
— when marriage counselling or partnership work has failed to move the couple towards new attitudes.
— when the one partner lives in terror of the other.
— when the children are also in terror.
— when the couple deny any interest in each other, mentally, emotionally or sexually.
— when unfaithfulness has happened once too often.
— when continued living together will break down the integrity of one or both partners.
— when the couple have tried more than once to resurrect the marriage, and their failure has proved that they cannot sustain the marriage.
— when the spiritual aspirations deeply believed in by the one partner are totally denied by the other with crushing effect.
— when estrangement has become irreversible.
— when love has turned to loathing.

# 24. The community of the future

Marriage is not the only form of committed relationship. Friendship has many different expressions. But it is the most comprehensive, encompassing all levels of normal relating. It is a school in which the participants are growing and learning all the time. But one of the problems of marriage today is that it is no longer supported by other kinds of bonding, to one's country, folk and clan: they are disappearing as emotional reference-points. All these affiliations and connections, which once afforded persons a 'home base' and orientation, are no longer meaningful. And marriage itself, as a last bastion of the old social nexus, is under stress.

Indeed it has to die as an institution: but then it will be able to resurrect as a process, a moving force that can fill out the sails of the individual as he manages his boat himself. Marriage is no longer a framework or a guarantee. Now it becomes a channel for progress towards discovery of oneself and of intimacy of a new kind. This new kind of intimacy has regard for the Self of the other, and generates every day anew the love that sustains a sharing of life and a maturing of a family of growing, authentic and unfolding individuals. Gone are the times when children should be moulded into a form prescribed by parents and governed only by inherited genes. Now the children shall become truly creative and able to work out their own moral principles as authentic persons. This they will be able to do if their parents have managed their marriage in a modern way, based on the new love, the sun-generated soul-force that is imbued with true feeling. All would then renew their enthusiasm for life out of an inner freedom that touches their own moral forces.

The distinction between the sexes goes deep. It is a biological fact that will not change until the human being ultimately evolves to a new state. The distinction engenders differences in soul make-up which can be overcome, because persons harbour both male and female characteristics in their souls: there it is a matter of achieving balance, and then the gender difference recedes. In the spiritual dimension the characteristics of woman and man become transformed into archetypal qualities. The great myths like that of Isis and Osiris indicate a deep duality of forces that arise from the highest order of the Spirit. This duality always calls for a third element, thus forming a triad or trinity.

In terms of the human spirit the archetypal Woman can be united with the archetypal Man, the Masculine power, by the working of Christ. Once this is achieved a truly sex-uniting relationship will be possible in the human being, in which the Female and the Male will know each other with understanding and selfless love. For that is the mission of Christ: to beget and nurture the power of love in the human being: not by melting the sublime principles of male and female into an undifferentiated whole, but by elevating these archetypal principles to become part of the heavenly order. This would empower humanity to come down to earth endowed with the faculty for forming community.

This sublime vista is found in seed form in the renewed sacrament of marriage, as celebrated in The Christian Community. Marriage does have a future, far transcending what we can envisage today. We can divine this uniting and harmonizing whenever we are filled with that sublime power which has been referred to in this book as *feeling*. And, more, this quality of higher unity will be experienced not only in marriage but also to some extent in all relationships. Through this we will be able to live in friendship and love with all our fellow human beings, through community engendered by the Christ.

Then all the trials that we encounter in the process of marriage and relationship will take on a deeper meaning: couples and their children will feel the exhilaration that comes from transforming problems into opportunities to become the new persons required in the coming age of brotherhood, Philadelphia. An endeavour of this significance could never be easy. With understanding and the overcoming of one's own smallness, the crises that threaten to rupture marriages and all other relationships could be turned to the positive, releasing new soul energy and generating a new wisdom of love.

The challenge of the coming millennium asks for a new kind of wisdom. Our striving for relationship is schooling us in this new wisdom. It has been the aim of this book to provide some guidelines to help us to find it.

# Notes

1. *On the Dignity of Man,* Library of the Liberal Arts, Indianapolis 1965, p.5.
2. See the opening passage of *How to Know Higher Worlds,* Anthroposophic Press 1994.
3. *The Third Force,* Frank Goble, Pocket Books, New York 1971.
4. We are using the word 'congruent' to mean speaking out exactly what we feel, without the need to hold back or cover up. We will say more about this in Chapter 17.
5. A reference to the book *Momo* by Michael Ende, Puffin Books, Harmondsworth UK 1984.
6. This is a reference to various findings which indicate that the two hemispheres of the brain function differently. The left hemisphere which controls the right side of the body, is logical, dealing with facts, associations and consequences. The right hemisphere controlling the left side of the body, is creative and intuitive; it works with totality and wholeness. The left analyses, the right synthesises. For an account of the left/right brain distinction, see for instance, Stephen Covey, *The Seven Habits of Highly Effective People,* Simon and Schuster, New York 1989.
7. Rudolf Steiner, *How to Know Higher Worlds,* Chapter 4.
8. Marilyn French, *The Woman's Room,* Virago Press.
9. Harriet Lerner, *The Dance of Anger,* Harper and Row 1986.
10. John Gray, *Men are from Mars, Women are from Venus,* Thorsons, 1993.
11. Rosalind Miles, *The Rites of Man,* Grafton Books, 1991, p.9.
12. See reference to fig-trees in J.G. Frazer, *The Golden Bough,* Macmillan, 1987.
13. Michael, Gagnon, Laumann and Kolata, *Sex in America: a definitive study,* Warner Books, 1994.
14. *Sex in America,* p.94.

15. *Sex in America,* pp.96f.
16. Henri J.M. Nouwen, *Reaching out: The Three Movements of the Spiritual Life,* Collins, London 1976, pp. 33, 35.
17. Paul W. Coleman, *The Forgiving Marriage,* Contemporary Books, Chicago 1989; Sergei O. Prokofieff, *The Occult Significance of Forgiveness,* Temple Lodge, London 1990.